PERSPECTIVE

Tara Knowles

I'm An Emotional Woman, **Not a Weak One**

Orders: Please contact www.perspectivebookshop.com

You can also order via the e-mail address Orders@perspectivebookshop.com

ISBN: 978-1-9196049-0-9

First published: 2021

Pintables from this book are available for download on www.perspective.com

PERSPECTIVE

I'm an Emotional Woman,
Not a Weak One

Tara Knowles

Dedication

This book is partly dedicated to every single soul I have ever encountered in this lifetime. Everyone has played their individual role; you were detrimental to my experiences at the time. As some of us can be women that are emotional, which can be frowned upon or seen as weak. When in fact my emotions have many times been my strength.

This book is dedicated to myself. My life journey has been a struggle, but I am proud of the things I've done and the person I've become. Writing about these things has been one of my greatest achievements.

Thank you to my daughter, my greatest achievement of all, who puts up with every part of me and accepts me for the crazy individual I can be. I love you. Thank you for supporting me, loving me and comforting me when I'm showing strength during times of weakness. For always being SO GRATEFUL and supporting me on my journey and living through certain sacrifices. I'm learning every day that without you, I wouldn't be half the super woman I am today. My Girl.

My Mum Sharon, thank you for always supporting my ideas and goals—no matter how mad some ideas are at times. She believes I can do anything.

To my Dad, who said I should write a book in the first place.

Thank you for believing in me when I doubted myself.

To my friends, who heard yet another one of my crazy ideas and supported it, not only with energy, but with their time and communication. Unusual situations and touchy subjects that were beneficial to discuss in my book, as well as for us all to personally grow and understand not only each other as individuals but, most importantly, ourselves. To Myles, Thank you for supporting any and everything I do, for listening and ignoring me when necessary. Forever grateful for the last 15 years of friendship – here's to 15 more !

PERSPECTIVE

To the Men I have loved. Thank you for both good and bad experiences I wish you happiness in everything you do.

Last but not least, thank YOU for Reading/Buying/Sharing my book! Thank you all for everything. I'm very grateful.

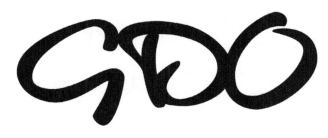

GREAT DAYS ONLY

A POSITIVE MOVEMENT

LONDON . UNIVERSAL

Contents

PART 1: THE ROOTS OF ANXIETY   **19**

Childhood anxiety and panic attacks   19

My first panic attack   20

Coping mechanisms   21

Internal and external feelings   22

Consequences   24

I thought I was weak   25

PART 2: PERSPECTIVE   **28**

To you who made me cry   30

Recognising when something is wrong   32

The love bomb   34

Perspective   37

But it was love at first sight   38

Intensity and power   42

Realisations and reflections   44

Questions   47

Hidden in plain sight   48

The danger zone   49

Unwanted transformations   51

The game   52

Testing the limits   54

Contents

The last straw 56

Intuition 62

Only in *my* head 64

After 66

Intention and me 67

I can't keep waking up like this 73

Questions and answers 75

PART 3: EMOTIONS **79**

Understanding our emotions 79

Emotions and mental health 79

Depression 81

Helping yourself 84

Confronting negativity 86

Under the rug 88

Processing hurt and pain 91

Worth 94

PART 4: GREAT DAYS ONLY **97**

The subconscious mind vs the conscious mind ... 97

Making every day great 98

Experience and learning 100

Contents

Health 105

Coping 108

Lying by omission 111

Toxicity 114

I used to have a temper 118

Managing my weight 120

Discipline 122

PART 5: THE AWAKENING **125**

Childhood bullying 125

Breaking down barriers 127

Thoughts 130

Understanding intent 134

Reactions vs responses 137

The mask 139

Shame vs embarrassment 142

Sometimes I feel like writing 146

Ibiza Mornings 148

PART 6: MANAGING OUR EXPECTATIONS ... **151**

Parenting: reality vs posing 156

Support and encouragement 159

Contents

Setting an example 161

PART 7: PRESSURE AND MANIPULATION **164**

The poisoned apple 164

The drone effect 165

Re-evaluating happiness: perception vs reality ... 167

Entertainment vs pleasure 170

Charm and manipulation 171

Conspiracy #ThePlan 174

Distant reflections 176

'Situationships' 178

Chemistry 182

PART 8: RE-EDUCATING OURSELVES **187**

The playground situation:
roundabouts, slides, and see-saws 187

School lessons vs life lessons 189

Learning through relationships 196

Adulting timeline 196

Pain 199

Back to basics 201

Recognising red flags 205

Contents

Lessons from sex 206

Rape, drugs, and alcohol 208

PART 9: RE-DISCOVERING HAPPINESS **211**

Breaking negative cycles 211

Reflecting lying in the field 215

Overcoming pain and finding happiness 217

Freed 218

Time the healer 220

Keep your heart 222

Distancing ourselves from drama 224

PART 10: HEALED PEOPLE HEAL **226**

Placing yourself 226

The world is in our hands 229

The pig story 235

Trees 238

Outline

In **Part 1**, I discuss where the negativity started for me, specifically in relation to the anxiety and panic attacks I experienced when I was young. **Part 2** outlines two significant relationships in my life and how they forced me to examine what I really wanted. **Part 3** delves into emotions and how our emotional state relates to our mental health. I discuss my own battle with depression and the coping mechanisms I developed to help me through those tough times. **Part 4** focuses on my turning point in life – a terrible summer when I discovered I wasn't the only woman in my man's life, and that my daughter had an unanticipated health issue. These things were my triggers, pushing me to make positive changes in my life. But to make these changes, I had to look back and be honest with myself about my past. This is the subject of **Part 5**, 'Awakening', where I examine everything I'd swept under the rug for so many years. **Part 6** is all about self-awareness and managing our expectations. We have to know ourselves and what we want before expecting others to give us what we want. Recognising pressure and manipulation is the main theme of **Part 7**, which explores the many guises pressure and manipulation can take, from guilt trips to charm. This chapter also discusses what I like to call 'situationships', where we fool ourselves into thinking that a casual relationship might turn into something more serious if only we wait long enough. Educating ourselves about what we want and expect from life is the theme of **Part 8**, which explores all those things that school often fails to teach – how to feel good about ourselves, how to make good life choices, etc. I also explore how different types of up-bringings can lead to the problems that many of us encounter in relationships – lack of practical support (cooking and cleaning), lack of emotional support and lack of respect. Finding happiness and removing things that get in the ways of happiness, is the main topic of **Part 9**. There are so many ways we can find our happiness; the journey is unique to each of us. Yet there are some common elements that we can all use to help us get there, whether it's talking, writing, or just taking the mental space we need to reflect on ourselves and our happiness. **Part 10** draws on one particular day in my life where I felt passionate about going forward, happy with where I was at, and full of understanding about all

the pain and hurt that had once been such a perma-
nent fixture in my life. This day had such a profound
effect on me that I decided to close my book with it,
leaving you, the reader, with the message: 'healed
people heal'.

INTRODUCTION

I wrote this book for two main reasons. The first is ca-
tharthic. I felt an overwhelming need to get my story
out of my head and onto the page. Doing this has been
a massive relief, lifting a weight off my shoulders and
clearing my mind. If you're someone who struggles
to talk about their thoughts and feelings, I can't rec-
ommend writing enough. The second reason I wrote
this book is to use my story to help others. People are
rarely honest in life about the dark times and negative emotions they've experienced. They're not often
spoken about, which can leave us feeling very alone. I
want to tell you my story so that if you ever feel alone
you may feel less alone. More than this, I want you
to learn from what I went through and find new ways
of coping with and approaching difficult situations in
your own life. Basically, I wrote the book I wish I'd read

PERSPECTIVE

when I was struggling with life. There have been times in my life when I couldn't see light at the end of the tunnel. When I couldn't even come to terms with how and what I was feeling. I was overwhelmed and encumbered by a feeling of powerlessness that prevented me from seeing my problems, let alone dealing with them.

I hope this book can be read with an open mind, and also used to improve your own well-being and potential. It's great to learn from our own mistakes, but even greater to learn from others. 'Each one, teach one', as the saying goes. Learning comes in many forms, but we are not always aware of what we are learning, or where to find what we are looking for. Sometimes it feels like it's too late to learn and that mistakes have already been made from which we cannot recover. I hope to show you in this book that this is never the case. Mistakes can always be learned from and can even be used to make you stronger and more resilient as you go through life. Tomorrow is another day. Before I started writing this book, anxiety rushed through my body. I knew I couldn't just include the good bits and leave out the bad. I had to give it all – the good, the bad, and the ugly. All of our lives are a mixture of these things. The trick is to use the bad and the ugly to make more of the good, which is something I'll discuss throughout this book.

Every day I have anxiety, before I do most things. Small things like going out can be easily made into a big deal and it's all internal. Everything starts from a thought. Then, it turns into a feeling. After that feeling, we are then stuck in between a thought (50k+a day). In which many are repeated thoughts. If we acted on every thought we had every day, I think the whole world would be sectioned for many different reasons. How often does the thought – the worry – and the thought of worry happen? The brain again protecting us. What if this? What if that? I would describe myself as emotional and sensitive, someone who wants to make others happy and laugh and do well in life. Some may not see me this way, and that's ok. There are several barriers and boundaries I've put up over the years, so not everyone gets to see that side of me. Some might see me on the defence, with a little attitude. Others might see me as someone who's always ready for confrontation

PERSPECTIVE

– even ready for a brawl. Either way, it's in knowing who you are and what boundaries you need to have to keep you safe. We also need to recognise that our boundaries can sometimes get in the way of healing and moving forward. Knowing when a boundary serves us and when it limits us is important and comes with self-reflection.

Hurt people hurt people. Healed people heal.

I was hurt for such a long time I didn't even realise the character I had shaped into. I had become a broken version of myself, someone who relied on hurting others to prevent others from hurting me. My defence became my lifestyle – no one would be able to take liberties with me again! In any way, shape, or form. I was a nice person until I wasn't. This book is about my journey from someone who was broken, to someone who found healing through self-awareness and, eventually, through self-love. By talking about the issues I faced and how I dealt with them, I hope to help you, the reader, with your own life journey.

PART 1: THE ROOTS OF ANXIETY

I want to start things off by exploring where my emotional struggles in life really began. To help you understand where I'm coming from, I'll give you a brief run down of myself: I was born and raised in South London, UK. I come from a mixed ethnic background. My dad is from St Lucia and I have English, Irish and Italian ancestry on my mum's side. My dad has nine kids, and my mum has three, including me in the middle. I have two sisters from my mum, one older, one younger, I'd say we have a pretty small family, until we're all in one house. My grandad (my mum's adoptive dad) is no longer with us, but he was an important part of my childhood and the only consistent man in my life. I spent nearly every weekend and every school holiday with my nan and grandad. It was on one of those weekends that things first started to go wrong for me which was when I had my first encounter with a panic attack.

Childhood anxiety and panic attacks

Growing up, I can't say I had any complaints. I had a great childhood. I didn't have many friends and I was

19

very quiet, but I wasn't unhappy. I was naïve to every-thing - life, dangers, emotions. I would say that I was rolled up in cotton wool, well-fed and watered, with not much to complain about. At least, that's how it was until I started having anxiety and panic attacks around the age of about 9 or 10.

My first panic attack

I can remember the first one as if it was yesterday. In fact, it's the clearest one to date. I was lying in my grandparents' front room on their black leather long seated sofa. It was dark and late. My nan was a head nurse at a care home, so she'd often work into the night and early hours of the morning. My grandad was a limo driver at the time and had executive jobs to take people to the airport (which was one of my favourite things with him – plane watching at the airport with the binoculars). He was on an airport run on the night my mind decided to go into overdrive.

I can't tell you exactly what I thought that night. It was so overwhelming that it felt as if I had forgotten how to breathe, which put me even further into a state of panic. The first thing I did was call my nan, who didn't answer. Then I tried my grandad, who was out on this VIP airport job (who books a stretch limo to the airport?). He answered with his usual "hey babe", but I was too hysterical to answer. I couldn't breathe, couldn't do anything, couldn't even speak. My grandad panicked and apologised because the whole limo could hear our conversation – this is when it started.

Coping mechanisms

Anxiety and panic attacks are actually really common, it's just that no one really talks about them, although this is beginning to change. Those experiencing these attacks often don't even realise what's happening to them. I couldn't understand what was happening to me for such a long time. Or maybe I should say that I didn't know where those intense feelings came from, what triggered them, or what would stop them. I was young, and to look back now as a parent myself, I realise just how sensitive I was to moods, feelings, and energies. They do say that kids are more aware of these things than adults, who tend not to notice them as much.

Anxiety took such a dominant role in my everyday life that it seems as though it was always there. I had to learn to cope with it in stages, but this wasn't easy when I didn't have anyone to help me understand what I was going through. I felt as though I couldn't do anything while wanting to do everything. I'd overthink things – even small things that shouldn't have mattered. It's normal to feel nervous about undertaking new experiences, like going somewhere you've not been to before, or talking to people that you've only just met. The trouble is, I didn't just feel nervous about these sorts of situations; they sent my anxiety levels through the roof.

Internal and external feelings

The strange thing is, my anxiety was rarely noticed by others. My shortness of breath, shaking hands, trembling legs, the sick feeling that swells in your whole digestive system – no one but me seemed to be aware of these things. No one has ever commented on how nervous or faint I look, or how I look as if I am about to vomit. I've never even had a general "are you okay?". This can only mean that I must look and seem fine to others. I gradually came to understand that this over-whelming feeling is only internal. I try my hardest in any situation where I feel anxious to remove myself from it. I can then explore what it is that made me feel that way in the first place. This isn't easy because when you're anxious, it's hard to think about anything else. Besides, thinking about what you're thinking isn't always healthy, as it can get in the way of life. Whilst no one would be aware of my anxious episodes or panic attacks, fear that someone would notice was often enough to stop my anxiety from escalating into a full-on panic attack. My fear of having a panic attack was so strong that I'd rather have had a fatal accident than experience one.

This may sound dramatic if you have not had a panic attack - and that's ok. The point of me explaining my honest emotions is to bring awareness to the thoughts and feelings people can have about panic and anxiety, even when the effects of these things appear invisible to others. Too often, these things are hidden beneath bravado. We all have egos to maintain, so we all like to behave as if we're ok. Admitting that we need help isn't a weakness, though sometimes it can feel like one.

Consequences

I feel like my personal journey with anxiety caused me to be avoidant, even when things hurt me or insult my soul, or when I knew someone else was wrong. I'm not saying I was never wrong, but there's a difference when it comes to other people's actions and intentions. Mine were never to intentionally hurt or upset other people, though this can certainly be an unintended consequence of trying to protect yourself.

I thought I was weak

I used to dislike being sensitive
It made me feel so weak
No control over my emotions
When at their highest peak

They'd keep me up at night
Angry, sad, then silent
I wondered what would be the push
Until I became violent

Then came the control
After sitting with my emotions
How long could this crying go on
Before I made an ocean

As waves would crash beside me
Whilst spraying me with sea
I never thought I'd be this deep
The drowning made me see

It isn't my emotions
It's how I view and see
It was all in my perception
And my reactions cut me deep

PERSPECTIVE

It was all so self-inflicted
You can't see at the time
By being all this sensitive
It's what really makes you shine

Embrace all of the feelings
Even ones that make you sad
We have to feel them all
They're not all bad

The joy is right beside us
Hidden in the smile
It's while we sit and socialise
And laugh along the while

It's when we be ourselves
With nothing to expect
The best lives are lived this way
With loads of self-respect

Being free from the ocean
Made me change my view
It's love and strength within us
That's oh so powerful

I'd sometimes sit and wonder
The thoughts that made me stronger
Embracing all the sombre
I thought that I was weak

Now I sit in strength
And look down at my scars
I could have made it simple
To release some of the bars

It was only then I realised it was all a dream
One that I can learn from
When nothing else can be seen

PART 2: PERSPECTIVE

This chapter explores my experiences of falling in love and renegotiating what I understand about love and what it should be. Three relationships really stand out for me. The first love – when I had my wonderful daughter - was maybe more of a misunderstanding and misinterpretation of what we thought love was and we just went with it and accepted it. My second love, which I hadn't been looking for, proved to be an important learning experience for me. To the third – who was the nail on the head to write this book, because surely... not all men are the same and operate the same way. Love at first sight and a blessing and a lesson all in one – wrapped up over 10 months These Intense and fast paced situations. I needed to understand the way we think and why we do things, look at our intentions and others' intentions as well. Why not just love and live happily ever after? Why make mistakes and then return with apologies? 'You don't know what you've lost until it's gone" is such a shame. Why does it have to take losing something that is great for us to realise it was great. Sometimes you can be the perfect package. But if the recipient doesn't know how to handle you, you will be mishandled and maybe damaged, depending on whether you were labelled fragile or if they even cared at all.

PERSPECTIVE

To you who made me cry

I never wanna ask
Never know what's wrong
Only get the vibe you're on
When you play us a song

In ways this act is childish
Communication is the key
Maybe it's the stuff you hide that makes
You be less free

If we shared all of our problems
And put them in a hole
If we plant them one by one
And see the seeds that grow

For each one that we sow together
Rewards it is we reap
It's just the process is for two
And not an individual streak

So, if you want to be alone
Just let me on my way
Because it's the way you dealt with me
That made me not want to stay

You kept me always wondering
Breadcrumbs to say the least
When I was empty and starving
You held the biggest feast

Without an invitation
You stopped communication
No urgent hesitation
A heart full of devastation

So, stand and watch me wave
This is my last goodbye
I couldn't stay and love no more
To you who made me cry

PERSPECTIVE

<u>Recognising when something is wrong</u>

Let's now place me at age 16, just leaving school. I've fallen in love, and everything in my life revolves around this first love. I wanted to spend all my time with him, plan my life with him. I loved him and was anxious that this love might be taken away. Even before I'd met him, I'd become a pleaser to avoid anxiety. This meant that anytime there was a problem, I'd want to do ANY-THING TO FIX IT.

At age 18, I had my daughter. At times, I did think that our daughter would be the gel that would hold us together. Now, there were three of us, our own little family. Except the emotional damage was taking its toll. I would be ignored in situations that should have been communicated, which led to a steady build-up of toxicity in our relationship. Living with someone who ignores you when there's a problem becomes increasingly difficult the longer it goes on. Not being listened to was especially difficult when I was doing everything that was expected of me – playing "miss perfect" housewife, dinner ready on time, house OCD clean, bath prepared, ready to hear about his day, our baby bathed, fed, and in bed. To have him come home late, not answering his phone to let me know when he'll be home. To be told, when he finally gets home, that he's been out with 'work colleagues'. As this was my first proper relationship, it took me a while to realise that our situation wasn't normal. I didn't know what relationships were, or what love was supposed to be, let alone self-love and respect. At such a young age, I was understandably naïve about these things. With all the good and bad that came from that relationship, it was nevertheless my bubble – one that I chose to stay in between the ages of 16 and 22.

Meanwhile, his world continued to revolve without me, even though he was at the centre of mine. All relationships with people are either blessings or lessons, and you'll get a fair few that are both, which is what lead me to write this book. After that first relationship, in which I had my amazing daughter, I stayed single and celibate for a year. Shortly after that, I stupidly decided to sleep with my long-term friend and work colleague. This was after a series of intense emotional events which I believe changed the way I looked at things - emotional clouding, as I like to call it. Though I made a poor decision, it taught me a great lesson - not to sleep with your friends, as the friendship can never go back to what it was (at least, this was my experience). Once you've crossed that line, you can't go back. If you've done it and have remained friends like nothing happened then I salute you. For me, I think my expectations changed - I went from expecting nothing to expecting everything from something that I initiated from the back of my emotional cloud.

The love bomb

A few months after this friendly encounter, I was then introduced to my neighbours' partners' friend. Yes, that's a mouthful! Let's call him Daniel. When I met him, I actually felt a bit insulted that he even felt like he had a chance with me. Not that I thought I was better than anyone. It was just that every time I saw him, he was a bit scruffy; wearing tracksuit and trainers 24/7, messy hair, and let's just say a job in "sales" (on the road). I was now 23, a mum, and had held a series of jobs from an estate agent to a receptionist to a sales advisor. By this time, I had completed school and college for veterinary nursing and even touched university for a term of science. I was now working as a loan underwriter, which I thought was quite a good job for someone of my age. I didn't expect to stay in this job 8 years later, but it enabled me to reduce my hours and focus on my social life - that's another story for another book!. Daniel came into my life slowly but persistently. Over a period of a few months, he made me feel like I was amazing, the best thing ever, the best girl he ever had. Now remember, at this point I'd been single and celibate for a year and I'd made the mistake of getting involved with a friend just a few months back. Daniel would pick me up from work every day, take me to eat everywhere and anywhere I wanted, and spend a silly amount of time on the phone with me. No one had ever wanted to spend so much time with me for nothing in return but my presence. It was nice. He was growing on me. The more time we spent together, the more we were falling in love. After a few months, It was time, I thought, to invite him into my home. I decided to phone him and tell him to pop round. As I'd previously made my intentions for inviting him around quite clear,

PERSPECTIVE

he was shocked by my advance. When he arrived, he was astonished to see me on the floor painting skirting boards. I loved my home and loved how it looked (plus I had OCD). But he wasn't impressed, he said 'nah, why are you on the floor?'. He ignored my sarcastic response and told me that he didn't want to see me wasting my free time painting. He said he'd have the skirting boards sorted tomorrow. Let's just spend time talking, he said – and that's exactly what we did! In that moment, he arranged for his friend, a professional painter, to come and paint my whole house the next day. The next day came and so did his friend with all his rollers and brushes, and off I went with Daniel in his top of the range car to a well known UK shopping outlet. He spent more on me than I had ever spent on myself or on anyone else at one time. With all the affection that went with it, I felt special and adored. He treated me so well I couldn't help but share my feelings about him with my close friends. It was too good to be true. He showed me that you should never judge a book by its cover. NOTE ; Careful what you share and who you share it with. Not everyone is happy for you. It took me a few years to get hold of that lesson.

Perspective

This relationship was, of course, the start of something that I sometimes wish I'd ended at this point exactly. However, as badly as things ended, I can't say I really regret my relationship with Daniel. Even bad things have a purpose in life. We both had a lesson in this. His was, 'you don't know what you've got until it's gone'. He will tell you himself to this day – I am the best woman he's ever had, and ever will have.

If I removed all the bad things from my past, I wouldn't be who I am today, not just in terms of personality, but also in terms of my strength, my passion, my understanding, my wisdom, and my personal growth and understanding. My brokenness has been part of my healing. All these things have made me become the person I am today. I also wouldn't have been strong enough to leave a future situation that led me to question the men I knew and to write this book. Ladies. We all got our situations – especially when love is blind or feels unescapable. You are not alone.

PERSPECTIVE

But it was love at first sight

We had had each other on socials for a few years, and even exchanged numbers on some occasions and shared a motivational video or two. This was in my GREAT DAYS ONLY PRIME so everything was great – My life had fantastic momentum.

Everything was working out for me; I had a photoshoot coming up for my brand, I had everything printed and models ready, all sorted, scheduled and planned.

I had some work that needed to be done at home, and had a few quotes – which were looking quite pricey! To be honest, I was thinking that for that amount of money, I needed to give the work to someone I knew, or at least a friend of a friend. Business supporting businesses was definitely my thing, and I would do anything to support my fellow business people. So, I sent out all job info to... let's call this one Emmanuel. From that day onwards, we were completely inseparable. Here we go again...

This one was intense from the get go. I feel like I can say I've experienced love at first sight. It was Saturday May 4th 2019; it was a great week. My nephew was born on the Thursday, I had a photoshoot lined up on Sunday and I had gotten everything in order from the models to the photography to the location and props.

My daughter had a tutor over the weekend. Plus, I had this home job (removal of stuff) to make room for other things for the business at home. It was a great week. Everything's amazing, I'm in a great space, mentally, physically. I weigh my lowest at this point – I look and feel great and amazing. Its 2pm – my daughter is at the tutor's. There was a knock at the door. I didn't even check the mirror to see what I looked like. I didn't think it was that type of situation. I open the door and the chemistry was undeniably unreal – clear as day for anyone to see, you would have thought we were long lost best friends reuniting. It was an embrace that captured all of me. One where you feel instantly safe, loved and kept all in one moment. The type of hug that will make you question every hug you have thereafter. "Hi", we both said while still in each other's arms rocking side to side. Talking into each other's ears like, "how are you", "it's been too long"... but we got there! Time just stood still, it wasn't awkward, it wasn't strange. It was just right. Like just at home, this embrace felt like it had lasted minutes, just holding and rocking. It was a love movie unfolding right before my eyes. The emotions you see being shown by people at the airport when embracing someone returning home after forever. I instantly became infatuated and interested. He had my full attention. This was a rare thing. Just imagine, after that whole hug and embrace, I soon find out that his brother was standing behind us the whole time with equipment. I didn't even notice! That's how crazy this whole scene was. Honestly, love at first sight. The connection and energy was something I've never felt before – sensationally powerful. I'm tall, but he must have been a whole 6'3. A whole huge structure of a man. My mouth might have even watered – even got something else wet. Based on social media and Whatsapp profile pictures I had previously seen, there was no way I was attracted to this man, plus we had each other on social media for so long that I didn't think that he felt that way about me either to be honest.

Neither of us had expressed anything like that. So here we are – he's got my attention.

As the job got done, we spoke about all kinds of things from the positive motivational videos I had sent him back in January, to my up-and-coming photoshoot the next day. As soon as a I knew it, the job was done. You know the saying, "time flies when you're having fun". I was indeed. My heart sank as we continued to speak, bringing the chance encounter to a close and making payment. This is going to end. I don't want it to end. Just being in his presence was powerful – his energy was amazing. I say that as an empath. Yet we said our goodbyes and that was it. I stand by my front door, breathe and just try to take it all in – trying to make sense of all of it. Smiling to myself, I reach for my phone. I think about messaging him, but I put my phone right back down, and finally give myself a look in the mirror. The little smirk I had on my face was amusing until I heard another knock at the door. It's him. I thought he might have left something. Nope, he was back to see me! He said "there's no way I can just leave like this! I'm missing someone like you in my life, I NEED someone like you in my life." I smile – he ended up staying for about an hour after the job. We discussed everything so freely like we were long lost primary school friends.

Intensity and power

From this day, until the beginning of 2020, he was my person. He sent me information to business events. He wanted to introduce me to people that I could collaborate with to enhance my shoe brand and also my personal brand and coaching. How could we develop this business idea – not only for individuals but also for other businesses? We did everything, not by force, just naturally. We created a business idea - a formula that could help other businesses profit and thrive. Win win right? We were together all the time, working all the time, creating all the time. Making money in between with both our businesses. I also worked part-time at my job two days a week to be able to support my business ventures – a solid consistent income. He would introduce me to new prospective clients that may need printing done. He would stay up all night and help me print. A few weeks later, when we established some business terms, we decided it would be better if we keep us quiet and not tell anyone that we were sleeping together, loving one another other and staying together 24/7. We both felt that people wouldn't take us seriously as a couple doing business. We wanted to keep everything professional. This is when I learned the term, 'don't mix business with pleasure'.

We both started a youth mentoring course that would help us better spread our business ideas - even if for free. Especially at events for children or some community projects. Not everything's about money – it's also about building genuine relationships. I know where I've come from, and what I've been through. I'm telling you at certain points in my life, I wish I had a vision board session when I was a kid! Not collages of flowers or nature. That's all good stuff – but we need educating on what we are eating and thinking more than what colour the leaves turn when they drop off the branches in autumn. Teach a man how to fish and he will eat forever - something along those lines.

PERSPECTIVE

We did family-oriented tasks like shopping, cooking and cleaning. Making the bed was so much fun, and a lot easier with two. I've never had this before, making the chores fun and then getting to eat and drink and binge watch or business plan in comfort. I was grateful and he knew it. Everything was perfect. I'd met his child. He'd obviously met mine; we had met each other's families – not purposely – but it was bound to happen since we were inseparable. Again, we were business partners right?

Realisations and reflections

He's had a holiday coming up, a birthday bonanza, and you want to do it big in Thailand with your boy! I was so for it. As far as I know, it was booked before we had met. The time was coming up and I'm doing the most as the 'woman in your life'. I thought, let's write a list of what he needs, how much money he will take and anything else he can think of? Holiday clothes and trainers, the amount of money to spend etc. I'd basically spent my next investment investing in someone who I didn't really know, and it's only after spending that money – which I got back in the end by the way – that I even began to think, 'hang on! I'm moving like a wife, yet he's not moving like a husband'. It's very much the same old pattern as before. I'm putting in 150% and someone else is putting in 25%. Plus, my well-trusted intuition was playing around with me. The day of his holiday comes – we speak, message and I send him safe flight wishes. I think and feel a few things: 'is he going with another woman?'. The one I suspected? But she just worked for him, or so he said. Then I felt a bit sad thinking about why we didn't plan to go somewhere. If he is really going where he says and with who he says. How would I even know. Whilst I await for a slip up on snap chat or on one of our phone calls. Which he had everything run smooth. Professionally infact,

He arrives safely, has a great time, social media's popping more than any contact with me, but that's fine. Plus, I think of another perspective; 'what am I like on holiday?'. Definitely not sending messages – just taking pics and doing what I want to. Ok cool. Allowing freedom. Me being moany about why he's not contacting me is going to encourage him not to contact me. Let me be understanding. We messaged everyday regarding business and I commented on his Snapchat uploads. A few days go by, and it's now his birthday. I send him a message – Thailand time. I sent a whole speech via message of what an amazing king he is and how much I love him and how much I appreciate him and how amazing he is. I miss him and cannot wait till he comes home me to hug me with he's whole being and I'm in bed alone. Oh, I miss him! He messaged me back saying that he's not having the best of times and that he's got some stuff going on and can't enjoy himself. Once again – another birthday ruined for him. Now, bear in mind, I'm also running his business, my business, my job that I hadn't yet resigned from while he's sunning it up in Thailand. Plus being a parent and also friend and family member. So many roles every day. Except, there were so many times where suspicion kicked in. Not only about the holiday, but overall, something wasn't right. We would have a good few days, and a few bad. It became a pattern that started to affect my mental health - much like how I felt in my first and second relationships.

Questions

Being ignored when I'm trying to communicate was a red flag I painted yellow, then green, and gave myself the go ahead. It was like I already loved him. I felt it deeply, as if it was a soul tie from a previous life kind of love. Except now he knew this through my words and actions – it's like he got it (me) and didn't maintain it (there's a part on this). But now I'm here, he's got me, he's comfortable. Then, a bit of emotional manipulation by starving me of attention then love bombing me with it all. Chill time, us time – Netflix and chill time. It was like alcoholics who hide what they do and who they are. It's the same with narcissists. I've not met a narcissist that admits they are one. Even if they possess so many characteristics and they are examples of their actions in real-life. They'll outright lie, and that's pretty much all that you can expect from them. It's a world of their lies and manipulation that gives them the kick of life that makes their world go round.

After me questioning him about the situation he may have faced, he became defensive, dismissive and rude. Blame me, tell me I'm being silly and making things up. It's all in my head. Then, love bombed me on his own accord once he feels like he's satisfied with how much hurt he's caused, for me trying to gain clarity to the situation I'm giving 150% and more to. For me, this is more than just fun – this is my life, my business, my reputation, and my responsibility. I have a young queen watching me. I'm a good example for some things and a bad example for others. There would be no arguments around her, but still. She's old enough to catch a vibe and knows me well enough to know my great days only streak is missing.

Hidden in plain sight

Being emotionally manipulated isn't an obvious move – it's like being in a big crowd then a huge smoke bomb is released into the crowd and you can't see shit.

You can't do much, you can only trust what's an arm's length in front of you. Even then, it's just you and your instinct and your thoughts, which can sometimes be helpful. But which one do you listen to and which one do you ignore?

The danger zone

This is a vulnerable danger zone, after thinking that you've upset the one you love or done something to them for them to ignore you. You feel relieved when it's over and things are back to some kind of normal. When the reality is its manipulation, they blame you then they're sorry and they're all over you. We fall for it. It's a weakness that all of us humans want. We want to be loved, heard and understood in whatever form we need. You feel relieved the bad times are over and the clouds are gone, and the sunshine is back. But you will now have to step on eggshells and become muted to some extent. Then put on your poker face like nothing bothers you in case you start something else that leads to more cloudy days. It's not worth it. To start the cycle again of the silence, waiting for the attention that sometimes never comes – unless they want something – whether it's monetary or sexual or just to meet their needs. But it's back on the round-about (also discussed in another part). The control and manipulation is dangerous and it's easy to lose our-selves. To lose a sense of who we are, what we know, who we know – it all gets lost somewhere and you feel so far away from everything and the only comfort and knowing is in them. That's where it's easy to be led astray or off target. When we put not only all our eggs in one basket, but we put everything including the future, hopes, dreams, aspirations with that person all in that basket and hand it over with a label called love on the front. I was faithful even though we weren't official. Everything else was official.

The amount of time we spent, the things we did, the family we introduced, the events we did together like Christmas and New Year's with our families, including doing activities with our kids, nieces and nephews. Complete family time. All the things us women hope for, the man who is ambitious, who has a business - a hardworking family man. But at one point or another, we have to ask whose vision is this and is it one sided? It's like I'm always trying to win him over or having to do something to get his attention. It all became very draining and started to affect many areas of my life.

Unwanted transformations

I resigned from my job - this wasn't because of him solely but just a consequence of how many things I was doing in one day and for my business. I was trying to build an empire off of all the things I had invested all my time and money in over the last 4 years. I had completely transformed myself inside and out to even be back here again, but I was weak and he had my love – which was my strength and also weakness. We would take on jobs where we worked together – some days working 20hrs+ on a few days a week over a couple months. But we had to keep the income coming in order to be able to flourish and achieve our plans. From buying a property to having a child and holidays to trips and retreats we would take and create. The business we would expand off the ones that we currently have. How we would work and then expand everything. I thought I had met my soul mate. My friend that I had introduced to him for business purposes messaged me one evening, sending me screen shots of her messages with him. Now, as far as he's aware, everyone knows that we are just business partners, but she's my girl, so I had previously informed her that this *was* my man, and if God hadn't sent him to me then I don't know who did. She was so happy for me and even gave me the down-low of men of this nationality as she was from the same cultural background.

The game

Cultral awareness is everything – I completed a course on this during one of my jobs. I think it's easy to assume everyone does things like you. I had this mentality for a long while - until life showed me differently. Life's best teacher – experience – or reading about someone else's is critical to having cultural awareness. I was super interested and also intrigued – one half of my ancestry is from a Caribbean country, and I have only been exposed to that side of my culture in terms of travelling overseas from the UK. So, to have first-hand insight was priceless. Anyway this one evening that she sent the messages they read something along the lines of, 'where do you live roughly, so we can hang out. What! I scroll down with my heart beating and hands shaking – friend still on the line. I feel like I can't breathe. I have to hold it together for my ego and pride. But oh my gosh! Really! My friend? You've sent messages and oh look - pictures. A whole selection of your top ten pics of last year. To say I was hurt, fuming and embarrassed would be really holding it down. I thanked her and asked her to not mention that she had even told me – this is what they call ahead of the game ladies – and where I failed. DON'T REVEAL ALL YOU KNOW. We don't want to play the game but, unfortunately, we are already in it. Don't show your whole hand and keep your poker face. I did none of the above.

My mouth watered. I felt the rush of sickness take over all other emotions. Anxiety had set in. I didn't want this to lead to a panic attack which was oh so familiar – I need to get some control over myself. I used some simple breathing techniques and had some fresh air while I processed what I was even going to call and say. This weekend he was taking part in a daddy-daughter time, and I really didn't want to interrupt that, but this held such a fire in my stomach, and it was the evening time. No more convincing or procrastinating - I make the call. No answer for a couple times then he calls back, that wave of anxiety comes back and I don't even know what to say when he answers. I ask him if he can talk and if he can't then to find somewhere. We need to speak. Now. This is the error – he's done the crime – and I have receipts! he's sent photos to my friend. I have photo evidence and also a phone call from the person directly minutes after he's sent these photos and messages. What more did I want to know? That is unacceptable. By me asking him any questions – what am I expecting to hear? (Whilst I'm on the phone to him he's gone to the chat with her and deleted everything, not knowing I have everything). There's nothing that he can tell me that is going to be good, so from when I've asked, it's like I've asked to be lied to. This is when I should have left. But God said girl, I got some more lessons yet to learn.

Testing the limits

So off I go painting them red flags green – I've completely skipped amber at this stage. For the first time ever, we didn't really speak that much that weekend. When he came back in the beginning of the new week, pissed that I had found out what he was doing the week before, discussing these things became a direct problem. The time had gone by and I wasn't as mad as I was, time is great for that, and the men in our lives usually know how long to give us to chill out and become more approachable. Enough time for us to miss them and think well that's happened now, is it a really big deal, it's over now, move on – great days only. But it wasn't just that, it was also the humiliation of my friend knowing this about my relationship. This gave me more anxiety and made me feel vulnerable not only on the inside but now also on the outside. This relationship and all the niggles were starting to take its toll on me.

Even though I was silently enduring emotional break-downs, I decided to stay. I decided to forgive and not forget, but to remind myself. Every time I saw him with his phone, the overthinking kicked in. I knew this was a big stab wound that wouldn't heal overnight. But cool, he didn't cheat, so it's not that bad right? Nothing happened, so it's not that bad right? I justified why it was ok to continue. He's probably right I'm just exaggerating, and being silly, right? It's like I had to question myself but still went against my better judgement. He was three years younger than me, my first experience of dealing with a younger man, but an old wise man in presence. But this situation wasn't even a fraction of what he was capable of, or what my intuition had been telling me all along. I just couldn't figure out what it was or how to even find out. It was the behaviours, the traits and the patterns that came from my last relationship that gave me the head start in this one, even though I was still being manipulated and deceived from the start. Intentions unknown.

The last straw

The last straw was on Sunday the 16th of February 2020. We woke up in my bed. I went downstairs and he was upstairs on the phone. Now from when he woke up, the whole vibe was just strange. For no reason – no communication, no discussing anything that may have pissed each other off. Nothing. But I felt strange. He asked me if I could go to the shop to get some tattoo cream for the tattoo he had sat through for ten hours the night before. Only 24 hours ago, I had gone to seven different shops to buy numbing cream. There's a whole vibe. My intuition is on fire, but again I can't put my finger on it. So, I think about what I can do. He's on the phone laughing and joking but he's rigid and serious with me, sending me to run his errands on a Saturday and Sunday morning. Cool. I start looking for my bank card with so much hurt in my stomach. I don't know what is going on. It's not been a year. I fully love him. But I can't do this all over again – especially after my last relationships. But based on what evidence am I leaving – it's like I was starting to believe I'm making it up. And maybe this is how things are supposed to be when you are in love. I've done this a few times now. I wanted this time to be the last. I thought he was my soul mate – we had good times and bad, but that's life no? It feels like you don't have any control, like your emotions control you. They control you because they hold your emotions. We then base love around these bad perceptions. Oh, I love you - so I'll stay. Shit man, this day I had had enough, and it had to be 'I love you, but I love me more'. Or it's going to get to toxic level 1000. I've been there and got the blue peter badge. I had an urge to become a detective. What can I do that's going to give me insight into what is happening – there's no one I can call and ask, I'm not going through his phone and I am certainly not asking him to create the next drama on a Sunday morning. I have a random strong urge to put my other phone on voice recording –. I then placed it in my bedroom, which was where he was. I leave the house, get what I need and come home. Hand over his cream – which I offered to rub in – he said he's not a child, and can do it himself. I forgot to turn off the recording and ended being over 3 hours long. He was acting super funny with me. I even became paranoid he had found out what I'd done and started to move differently because of this. I couldn't understand what it is that I had done to make him so upset with me for no reason. It wasn't long before he said he had a meeting regarding property stuff and he's going to leave. I wasn't invited to this meeting – being business partners. I found this suspect. We had always discussed prospect business ventures, and property was top of the list. It wasn't until he said that maybe he should leave his vehicle at mine and then I drop him home. I had a new bed delivery coming later that day – I just wanted to stay home, chill out, eat some food and plan the week for the businesses. But this made me feel better, him asking me to drop him home then potentially drop him there, thinking that he wouldn't be going to do no dirt and I'm dropping him home then he's going and then coming home to me and the vehicle that's parked outside my house. What could he possibly do? Unknowingly to me, I was about to find out. When he left that day, I had no idea the decision I was about to make after hearing what I was about to hear. It's not that I wanted to necessarily hear the calls – I respect privacy – but I wanted to find out what it was he was hiding so well. A few calls were made – and the majority of them were on loud speaker. First comment when I leave my house is this girl man – she's so inner. This is cheeky but thank you intuition, I'm not painting these flags – if anything at this stage I need a different tone of red. First caller doesn't say much, but it seems like a round of calls with ladies for the good morning calls – not even messages - calls. He keeps it short and sweet and keeps moving – talks about what a busy and productive day he's got lined up until the call made to a female who asks a lot more than the others, "what time" He responds with "I need to shower, sort out something, then I'll be there, but makes sense if I get a cab to yours from mine." This is it. There's nothing more here – it has been confirmed. I can't breathe, I don't know what to do, I feel sick. I'm weak and numb. I feel embarrassed to even share this with anyone. I feel heartbroken – a whole wiz of memories like a flippagram, from Christmas to New Year's, to our plans and future. I feel like a wrecking ball just pounding my whole body slam dunk. That's it – it's confirmed. We're over. As there were so many red flags that I had painted. I had to think back to the end of the year 2019 and we were going through some hard times. The hard times really show you someone's real character – especially if all you do is love, adore and support them, whilst on your own mission. I was in such shock. I had to call someone, I called my friend and explained to her everything I'd heard on the voice note. She said, "I'm coming around". I literally stayed in the same spot in tears sending messages then eventually blocking him when she got there, and I decided: this is it. Where can we go from here? I'm not doing this again; I don't deserve this. All I did was love him. Why wasn't I enough? What is it about me? Is my body not enough? Is it the way I look? Maybe I need a bigger bum like he hinted on more than enough occasions. It took me a long while. But it's none of the above, unfortunately these men don't know what they have got until it's gone. Or don't know how to handle such a great package. So, when being mishandled, it's not about you – it's about them.'

After a couple months, the woman he worked with, the one I suspected all along, had reached out. It turned out – he had done the same kind of thing to her. But told us both contacting each other would be detrimental to business. A compulsive liar a true narcissist. That birthday holiday he didn't actually go with her, he went with another woman, except this was a whole another girl I didn't even know about. How? He was with me 24/7 for months on end. I didn't actually find out about this until I had spoken to the other 'business woman', who had disclosed everything. That's also another thing; ladies don't be mad at the other woman (depending on the circumstances). Most time, it's the man that puts us in these situations in the first place. In fact, everything that my intuition had given me whether a feeling or a sign - it was correct, I just couldn't prove it. The conversations that me and the other business women had with each other was healing for us both. There was good time and bad time with him for us both. But at end of it all we are just two women who loved the same man. Even for he's sister – who I'd like to think I made a great relationship with and fell in love with the whole family. They all knew – and even then what can we do – family first right? I send them love and light.

Intuition

All this time my intuition was telling me something was wrong, and he made me out to be crazy. That's an absolute liberty. I can wholeheartedly see how things like this turn people mad. Or lead on to them doing serious things to themselves or others. I didn't get to that stage with this - I nipped this in the bud and took back the control and let that build over the time I had him blocked from everything. Then it's the process of eventually deleting everything. The everyday memories. Being unable to sleep. Or not feeling capable of dealing with the standard day. Whilst the whole world goes around so does the pieces of my heart that were shattered in my ribcage.

I would have some seriously bad days. Days where I had major anxiety and I didn't know one hour of emotions to the next. 24 hours in one day is like forever when you feel like this. That real heartbreak that kills your appetite or that makes you eat in comfort. With us eating shit and in turn feeling like shit. Potentially going from one issue to another. The domino effect. Everything affects everything. Everything is connected. It's just figuring out our own way of life.

PERSPECTIVE

Only in *my* head

You made me feel inadequate
You made me feel the pain
You once said that you loved me
I told myself again

I held on to the memories
The laughter and the hugs
Each tear of mine was pouring
As if it came from jugs

My heart I think it's open
My heart I think it's clean
It's only when it comes to hurting back
I see it's in deep need

The safety latch is broken
With only light, it can be seen
It's when I ended up in there
The memory made me see

It wasn't what you showed me
It wasn't what you said
It was a vision of mine
But only in *my* head

My heart became dependant
On love it thought that mattered
Not thinking that it's worthy
Now a vision that's shattered

It was there all along
It even had a song
Now a memory I see
That I just want gone

Was it just me?
It's clear to see!
I hope you'll be the best you can be
For my laughs
In-between the graft
Its' truly you that lost out fast

PERSPECTIVE

After

It took a year to build myself back and better to what I lost. "I'm back and I'm better" – word to Bryson Tiller. But it was also the driver for me to write this book. I've been here before, in these 'situationships', a few times now not even just me, but so many men and women. Yes women can be just as bad as men in all aspects. I found when I shared my experiences people actually understood or were able to relate and in turn also able to share their experience without the shame I had. I was already laid bare - it's like there was some kind of man code I didn't know about, nor did the other women or men. What is this man code and how do I find out? What are these overwhelming emotions and when did I even get them? I need to go to the men that I could really ask. I called my dad and ex-brother-in-law and a few fellow friends. These men once were the ultimate game players and compulsive liars with women all over the place and not even loving any of them or having any real intentions. Other than the kitty. To be able to sit and ask why? Us women have so much to lose and all we do is fall in love, get some dick and everything starts to fall apart... Not in all cases, but how many successful relationships have you had. 'Had; meaning they were not successful if you're not still in it. Or are they because you learnt something and was able to take on the new learning – or the old habits and traits from the last person on to the next. After many failed attempts at this, who do the women eventually become? The woman who is always with a new man every Christmas. Or every few months. Do we have kids? Do we introduce them? If they're going to be around, it makes sense to, but there's also so much that comes with that. Someone can be great with kids and still have ulterior motives, heck! Someone can be fantastic with kids and don't ever see their own. We still have to be aware and protect our kids. This now leads to intention and motive.

Intention and me

I always use to question why someone wanted to be with me. What was it about me, I didn't feel worthy, so I would tolerate what I felt worthy of? I was actually unhappy for so many years and I didn't even know. I mean I knew, but it wasn't something that was clear,

PERSPECTIVE

you just get up and keep it moving. The days go by and the next ones come. I didn't think about me, or what made me happy, or how much money I wanted to make, or what kind of woman I aspired to be. I was just lost. Misunderstanding and misinterpreting life and emotions, feelings and situations that arose – there's nothing new under the sun, but there is a first time for something that happens to you. What's their intention and what's mine. Now, I use this for everything, in business, personal and new people. I like to be direct and to the point. I am not one to beat around the bush. I'm more likely to burn it down and go directly to the source. When we know and understand someone's intentions in our lives, it makes everything so much easier. Everyone knows where they stand. Whether it's in a relationship and they can't really see them being with you. Why waste months of time and energy and emotions to then know. I feel that's because the intention was either uncommunicated and assumed or from the get-go, one sided intentions were in full force and you were none the wiser - just another victim of this serial sexual predator, among God knows how many others. The same can also go for women, I'm not binding this to one gender. After asking an array of questions on many different occasions, some very random like "Hey dad, so all these women that you had sex with, and even the ones you've created children with, did you ever love any of them – and was there anything they could have done to have kept you to themselves and reigned in your habbits with other women?". To which he would respond "Hmm, well Tara, that's an interesting one". Then we would have a pause, then a couple ad libs, then eventually after genuine thought he would answer "Well actually, I've only ever loved three women." Wow. What – so you have 9 kids, 7 baby mums and a countless number of lovers, (I'd be ashamed myself to even attempt to put a figure) and you've only ever loved 3!! The number of women that would have loved him is countless. Wanted to be that ride or die, or everything for you, buy you everything and anything to keep you around – people do that when buying things.

Some men and women think that when they have brought a gift or provided a certain amount of stuff that they have some control over you. I think this is cheeky.

PERSPECTIVE

I can't be bought, but at the same time, let me know what this is before I start investing into a liability. We only want to invest into assets – not just monetary, but in ourselves and also in people around us. If we water the plants and water our people with goodness – the love, the care and the support when it's needed - that builds you up, that keeps you going. That's an investment, that's what money can't buy. My dad was honest with me, and I couldn't have been luckier. He was able to tell me all the tricks all before they even happened, so as it started to unfold before my eyes, my dad became my mentor in how I now get out of this with my heart still somewhat beating. With everything I've invested into him, my time, my money, my business, my home, my family, it's the laughter and the good memories that get you. But when you look deeper at that memory and you scope into that day, that was maybe a ten second moment out of a 24 hours which actually was an unknown roller-coaster with full of ups and downs and trying to ensure we are ok and I'm walking on egg shells. So, really, out of the whole day that 10 seconds of us laughing really hard at something was just an exaggerated feeling within myself because of the whole rest of the day had gone. You start thinking that you will never find someone to laugh like that with again. Or to cry with, or to share the most vulnerable things about yourself with. To literally lay yourself bare. It was the most open I had ever been with any man – in the shortest time – compared to my previous relationships that had lasted years. I was more comfortable in what I would say, and do and be more myself, and be open to trying new things – even to make him happy. Again, the pleaser in me.

In life, the ying and yang of a giving person and a receiving is interesting. Look around you. Who are you? The giver or receiver? Some do great at being both. I'm a great giver, I'd give my world in some instances. But I'm a terrible receiver – due to my previous thought process I thought that because someone brought me something, and now if there's a problem I can't now be honest and say what's on my mind. I have to be nice and polite, grateful and hold back anything I might have to say or ask, and I just don't know how to do that well. I'd rather not be brought nothing and be able to say what's on my mind then no one has got any control

PERSPECTIVE

over me or can't hold anything they've done for me or brought for me. As a result of this, I created something within myself where I became reliant and more inde-pendent and achieve everything by myself. It might take me longer but I'm good I've got this.

How many of us have been brought something to cover up something else – we then are brought a gift, or sent flowers and then we can't really go mad or be suspect without hardcore evidence.And they do the whole love bomb, gift bomb and you now do what – reject it – I've done both. At that point, it's more the ego,.

I can't keep waking up like this

I can't keep waking up like this
My mind is in array,
My heart aching from everything.
I don't know if I can stay

I don't feel calm and centred
Unbalanced is the word
I feel anxious, sad and emotional
I wish I was a bird

To fly and sore though everything,
I might ask to be a bee
To build the might to sting you
The result in killing me

I don't know how to deal with this
You'd have to *overstand*
Or understand so selfishly
It's not part of the plan

Understanding each other's visions
For comprehension was the key
Out of everyone in this big wide world
You did this to me

PERSPECTIVE

You took complete advantage
Like they say when love is blind
But you covered up nearly everything
Then lied and said it's fine

They say don't take it personally
For it's not about us
But just a mere reflection of them
Like with a passing bus

It hit me more than double
Like boxers in the ring
Except you tried to play me
But I took the win

Questions and answers

My relationships have made me ask the questions, 'What is life?' 'What is love?' Everyone I've asked these questions to in the last year or so has had a completely different answer. This is probably because we all experience love and life in different ways. My own approaches to love and life have changed over time, shaped by the various challenges and situations I've faced. We all know what the words 'Life' and 'Love' are. We can all say them, but do we know what they mean? Do we act on them? Only when we critically assess what these words truly mean to us can we incorporate them into our lives in positive, fulfilling ways.

To me, love means all of the following:

Free and honest

A feeling of connection

Kind and caring

Helpful and supportive

Laughter and smiles

Hugs and comfort

Making great memories

Communication and understanding

PERSPECTIVE

When the following things start to creep in, then you have to question if what you have is really love:
Hurt and worry
Deceit – misrepresenting truth (including cheating)
Heartbreak
Stress and anxiety

We all want love; we all want a loving relationship in which we are understood. Sometimes we want these things so much that we fail to recognise when what we are receiving is a lack of love. Love hurts, but understanding when that hurt is a normal part of a relationship and when it isn't, can be tough. It's a grey area, which is why so many of us get stuck in unfulfilling, unhappy relationships. We have to remember, we deserve happiness. When that happiness is fraught with those negative emotions and behaviours outlined above, then you have to question if it's the sort of love you really want. The aim of this book is to give an understanding of how we can grow and heal as we move through our lives. Some of what I say may seem like simple common sense to some. If you are already comfortable and happy with who you are and what you've achieved, lucky you! But for those who have struggled to overcome a difficult past, the road to self-love is often a long one, and finding that road in the first place isn't easy. By taking you on my own journey, I hope to show that it is possible to use our experiences – good and bad – to become stronger, happier, and more resilient. If you can relate to what I'm trying to do here, and have your own story to tell, I encourage you to share it. Our personal experiences can be used to empower other women and even some men who experience similar things, helping them to cope with whatever challenges they face. The more stories we get out there, the more likely it is that women will find something they can relate to. It's all easier said than done. But self-love is a powerful process and journey, and one that is worth telling. Life situations will have you questioning everyone and anyone within your vicinity. We can only learn so much from our own experiences – that's why we crave other people's stories. Finding the right story for us can be a challenge. There are so many books out there (millions, in fact!) that finding what we're looking for can be like searching for a needle in a haystack. But the more we read, the more

PERSPECTIVE

we increase our understanding, and the more we might even find the courage to write our own stories down.

PART 3: EMOTIONS

Understanding our emotions

Our whole life is centred around our emotions, yet we are rarely taught how to recognise and deal with them. When thinking about emotions, it's useful to consider the following questions:

What are they?

How do we control them?

Why do we have them?

How many are there?

How are each of them supposed to make us feel?

What does mental health have to do with our emotions?

Emotions and mental health

If we understood our emotions, we would also have a better understanding of mental health. If you are human, and you have a mind, then you have mental health. Like our physical health, our mental health is something that needs care and attention. It can also require healing, whether in terms of self-care, reaching out to others, or even medical intervention. For some people, mental health is something they don't need to think about very often. For others, it can feel as though their mental health is out of control, negatively impacting all areas of life. Even though we know much more about this issue compared to a few years ago, there remains a stigma around the world of mental health. But we nearly all experience it at one point or another, whether we admit it or not. Here are some of the signs that can indicate poor mental health:

Behaving out of character

Feeling lost

Feeling like you have no control

Constant sadness

Overly emotional

Feeling anxious

These feelings stem from our mind trying to cope with various emotions. When we don't understand, or are not aware of, what's going on in our heads, it's hard to process what it is we are actually feeling. This can lead to a feeling of suppression, holding things in, not talking about them—a roundabout of thoughts.

Depression

Possibly the biggest stigma around mental health relates to depression. But depression isn't a curse to be feared, it's simply a mood disorder. If depression is a mood DIS-order, how do we get our depression IN ORDER? How do we know we are depressed? I think for everyone it's different, although there are a common group of symptoms and traits to look out for. For the purposes of this book, I'm going to focus on my own experience of depression. My mood pattern and behaviour went something like this:

I don't want to leave my house or do anything

I don't want to eat well. I want to comfort eat

I don't want conversations

I don't want to be around anyone

I feel anxious

I feel weak

I feel broken

I feel unworthy

I question every single thing about myself.

It's important to know what is making us feel like this. A thought comes before a feeling. Therefore, we must

PERSPECTIVE

think about what makes us 'Dis-order'. Recognising the cause is the first step to getting ourselves 'In-Order'. I made a list of what was making me depressed, and came up with the following:

I am depressed about:
My weight
My job
My relationship
Family stuff
My health (physical and mental)
Finances
Debts
My responsibilities/commitments

The list is endless. In daily life, there's loads going on and usually, regardless of the circumstances, you have to keep going. What else is there to do? But I noticed that 'keeping going' was taking its toll, resulting in behaviours that didn't feel like me.

My depressive behaviours and reactions:

Snappy and short with people

Cry by myself, to myself

Feel sorry for myself

Question myself

Ask 'why me?' I have been a good person

Dwell on how other people treat me

In these situations, we have to do the opposite of what we 'want', or what the disorder wants. Let's take a look at how 'disorder' is defined, which is how a lot of mental illnesses are defined, as a disorder.

If you look at the definition of a disorder the following words come up: disarray, chaos, disorganisation, clutter, confusion, a mess. This is exactly what I would say I was. A mess. And, to be honest, a bad one. A big bad mess. I felt as though no one could help or understand me. No one knew what I was going through, I was overwhelmed with every area of life and that light that the end of the tunnel was looking dim. My shame at how I was feeling meant that I couldn't tell anyone what was going on inside. I tried to distract myself, to get myself to a point where I had to motivate myself. Since I'd identified that my weight was part of what caused my depression, I thought this would be as good a place as any to start. I'd do things like find an image of an amazing body on Instagram and put it on my screensaver as motivation to lose weight. I'd visualise the body as mine and focus on how to make that vision happen. I'd plan the week out, being careful not to leave too much spare time, since this would often lead to falling back into a depressive mood. You know when you feel like you don't want to do anything? That's when you have to do everything - within reason, of course!

Helping yourself

Get IN order! Sometimes we just need to sit with ourselves. No phones. No TV. No music. No talking. Just you and yourself. How often do we do this? Not often, for me. Grab a pen and paper and get your thoughts out of your mind and on to the paper. This will help you to let go of those negative emotions – blame, shame, guilt. It can also help you to brainstorm or mind map the problem, situation or idea. The crucial thing for me was realising that I couldn't wait for someone else to help me. I had to take responsibility for my mental health and find a way to deal with it. Of course, if you have people around you to reach out to, you should absolutely do that. You don't have to go through depression alone. But reaching out in the first place requires you to acknowledge your mental health and take responsibility for it. You've probably heard the saying, 'You can only help someone who wants to help themselves'. We have to make that decision for ourselves. There were times where I was feeling a bit sorry for myself. I wanted to blame the world and the people who were around me for what was going wrong in my life. I came to the conclusion that this was transferring my problems onto another person instead of taking responsibility.

Blaming others can feel like the easy way out, but it also leaves you helpless, since you can't control those other people. Taking responsibility means taking control. Making the decision to take responsibility for your life is a fantastic achievement and will leave you feeling strong. Greatness comes from the worst of times. Instead of 'why me?', ask yourself how you can make a positive change. We all have wallowing days, but it's important to keep going.

Confronting negativity

When I was younger, I heard many expressions that I didn't actually understand. One that I had long forgotten about came to me recently: 'Sweep it under the rug'. This applies to so many things. I'm sure we can all think of something we have swept under the rug. How many things have we been hurt from and haven't dealt with? Sweeping things under the rug is only a temporary solution – it doesn't get rid of our problems or resolve them. Another expression that's always stuck with me is 'better late than never'. Sometimes it can feel as if it's too late to change something, like once it's happened, the opportunity to resolve or learn from it is gone forever. However, the saying 'better late than never' reminds us that it's never too late to clear out that rug and heal. Write all those buried issues down, acknowledge them. Cry them out and release them.

Free yourself and get rid of that rug. Or at least be aware of what's in there and deal with it one step at a time for your own process of healing. But you have to at least acknowledge it.

PERSPECTIVE

Under the rug

My heart's in need of healing
It hits me every time
When I hear your favourite song
Or taste your favourite wine

It gives me that nostalgia
Of memories in the rain
When we would laugh and turn around
and laugh out loud again

These memories here are hidden
Thrown under the rug
Like everything else, we hide under there
Except we need a hug

A hug to feel we are worthy
A hug to feel we are loved
It's what all of us humans want
It's just to feel enough

Enough to say we're happy
Enough to say we're sad
Enough we have to be US
Before we share the bag

The bag of stuff we carry
Just like the hidden rug
Least hidden is a lie I think
When it's as clear as shrubs

This mountain's overwhelming
The rug is at its peak
I wonder if we look in there
We will find what we all seek

It's all the stuff we have been through
Even when it's bad
And all the stuff that hurt so much
That made us so fucking sad

We have to stay a while
and dig a little deep
No avoiding it no more
I told you it's at its peak

The mountain's here to test us,
To make us strong again
We have to see what's in there
To trust and learn again

PERSPECTIVE

When we reach the peak
and look back around
I realise it was only me,
And it was me I found

Processing hurt and pain

We all experience hurt, rage and pain at various times. These emotions take up a lot of energy, and that energy can be used for better, more positive things. Easier said than done. It's the hardest work you will do that we try to avoid by escapism or any other means to distract us from the process.

You can create a stronger, better you. No one wants to REALLY hear this however, because the alternative can feel much easier: giving into negative emotions is easier than overcoming them, but only in the short term. If you give into them, they never really go away, but if you make an effort to overcome them, you won't have to deal with them nearly so often. Someone I asked about handling hurt and rage replied with this common phrase: 'If you can't beat them, join them.' I replied with another common phrase: 'Two wrongs don't make a right'.

Meeting rage with rage doesn't resolve anything. Rationally, most of us know this, and yet we still find ourselves using anger as a defence mechanism in difficult situations. Does it make us feel any better? In the short term, it can do. But in the long term, it not only affects your mental health, but your physical health. High blood-pressure, heart problems, and much else, can result from giving in too easily and too often to anger and rage. Committing to not giving into those negative emotions isn't enough on its own. You also need to think about how much you're willing to expose yourself to those emotions from other people. How often have you put up with being shouted at or otherwise disrespected? Doing this is a way of protecting ourselves; we ride out the storm, hoping another one won't come along any time soon. We tell ourselves everything will go back to normal once the storm is over.

Negative emotions used to dominate my life. When it became too much, I had to make a choice: my relationship, or myself and my happiness. I chose my happiness, even if that means being alone or settling for what I need and not what I want. I thought I just wanted you. But I didn't just want you. I needed you, I needed you to return my love. Show me affection. Give me the loyalty I deserve. Show me I'm important to you. You gave me coldness. Some days full-blown sunshine. Some days you left me out in the rain even though I was in your arms. I deserve love, honesty, and communication. I won't settle for anything less, and I'll do my best to return all I'm given. I am definitely not perfect and will never pretend that I am. If you ever at any point had or have this perception about me, it's all yours.

I have flaws. I have insecurities. I have fears. I have doubts. I have negative moments. I am human. I experience as much as the next person in terms of emotions and feelings and insecurities. Recognising these things and working on them is something we should never stop doing. They won't ever completely go away, but they can be managed and controlled, and removed from most of our experiences.

You are you, and everyone has a past, and also a choice for the future. This is ultimately down to us.

PERSPECTIVE

Worth

I deserve a true love
Not no manipulation
I've had all this before
It's only devastation

One that cuts right through you
Not only with a knife
But one that makes you look upon
The whole of your damn life

Will all that you've experienced
The things that made you grow
If only you saw this one coming
You would have let it go

We can't predict the future
But we can make a change
Just take some time to sit it out
Your life is not a game

So, when you feel you're played with
But you are not a doll
Remember who it is you are
and it's a choice to grow

We can take on all the lessons
And everything they teach
But if we don't learn from them
That's failure at its peak

We have these life experiences
To hurt and give some pain
But when we look out to see the sun
We only see the rain

This isn't just a poem
It's a message just for you.
If you've read and got this far
It may be about you

We all have a life journey
One where we want peace
And happiness is vital
It claims the missing piece

We search out of discomfort
Uneasy by the pain
All that manipulation
Made you weak once again

PERSPECTIVE

This is one day of many
The best is yet to come
But if you see yourself in this note
I'd say goodbye and run

PART 4: GREAT DAYS ONLY

'Great Days Only' is all about finding ways to make the day worthwhile regardless of what else might be going on - relationship drama, family drama, life drama, financial drama, and so on. The first step is being aware: aware of yourself, your behaviours, your thoughts, and of how you react or respond.

The subconscious mind vs the conscious mind

When it comes to the subconscious, we are taught the basics, but not the essentials. It is found the average human being has about 12,000 to 60,000 thoughts per day. 80% negative and 95% are repeated from the day before and the day before and the day before.

So how do we get new thoughts? How do we change our thinking process?

The answer is, we create them. Our conscious mind is always out to protect us and is on the alert for any danger so that it can tell the rest of the body to react. How we react and respond is linked to our mental health and varies from one person to another.

PERSPECTIVE

Making every day great

This is when people lose faith in things like the Law of Attraction. You can't expect everything to work itself out if you just meditate, say some affirmations, and be grateful. Making positive change is deeper than that. It's literally an everyday lifestyle. But you still have to do things to get what you want. Happiness and fulfilment won't appear out of thin air.

Go back to those basic questions about yourself:
Are you happy?
What makes you happy?
Are you earning what you want to earn?
What do you want to earn?
What do you want your body to be like?
What do you want to achieve for yourself?

When are we ever asked this stuff, and on the rare occasion that you are - how often are you able to answer? And honestly, at that. Being honest with yourself isn't as easy as it sounds. It is often much easier to pretend to yourself that you're happy than it is to confront negative thoughts and feelings. What is

'Happy'? You can't really get a straight answer on this because, as with the words love and life (discussed above), everyone has a different view on happiness and what it means. The definition given above can only take us so far. As you can see, happiness can refer to a whole host of positive feelings, but our unique take on happiness doesn't have to perfectly match the dictionary definition. Because there is no 'correct' answer, this means that happiness is a matter of perspective, and perspective can be changed. Everything happens in life for a reason, and it's when we change our perspective on what we experience that we become free. For myself, this means that what used to control me no longer does. I control how I respond to anything in life. This doesn't mean that I never make mistakes or act in ways that I regret, but it does mean that I'm aware that I control my behaviour – that what I do is up to me. As much as I try to be positive, I sometimes give way to negativity. I have moments and days where I struggle, and that's why I created a whole lifestyle from saying, 'Great Days Only'. This saying enhances how I see each day. Instead of focusing on how terrible a particular day was, I focus instead on what I've learned from that day. How did that negative feeling or experience drive me towards something better? Can the things that went wrong today be avoided tomorrow and the day after?

Thinking in terms of Great Days Only means that no day is simply 'bad' or 'wasted'. As long as we've learned something, we can class it as a great day – a day that added to our life journey. Turning negatives into positives is going to be a common theme throughout this book. As you'll discover, doing this isn't about clicking your fingers and expecting things to switch from bad to good. It's about recognising and understanding those bad things, taking control of them, and making them work for you. Hurt and pain are great drivers – depending on the direction they're driving you in. All journeys towards self-love start with some kind of trigger, and we all get our drive from somewhere.

Experience and learning

Nearly four years ago, my daughter was diagnosed with Type 1 diabetes. At the time, I didn't know what it was, and thought it was due to 'diet and lifestyle'. So why does my healthy six-year-old have it, I wondered. I soon realised that Type 1 diabetes is not the same as Type 2, which can be reversed through diet. It was shortly after my daughter's diagnosis that I came up with my new saying, 'Great Days Only', which was about to change my outlook on life, and on other people's lives. What started as a frightening health issue with my daughter transformed, over the course of a few months, into a more positive outlook on life and health for both of us. This would lead to a new business venture and, eventually, to a book about everything I was able to do with the business – from vision board workshops for adults and kids, to attending events to discuss mental health. I ended up mentoring clients for both personal and business advice, with a focus on clients who aspired to the manufacturing side of business. Or those who wished to enhance their reality with vision boards and plans and goals for life. From my first business with shoes, I had great overseas connections and developed strong business relationships with everyone I'd worked with in this sector. I learnt a lot and discovered a lot. These things that I created – from my shoe business to 'Great Days Only', all came from something I had in me internally. But life experience – with pain being the most significant pusher – caused me to lead my own way, to create my own path. Now the mission was freedom. Not only financial freedom but also the freedom from my own negativity. But at the time I didn't know any of this – didn't know what great things my future held. In the time leading up to her diagnosis with diabetes, I was overweight (20 stone), as well as very unhappy, angry, rude, hurt, in debt, lost, misguided, depressed, and generally just going with the stress of each day. And then some. So to see a six-year-old be able to prick her finger and inject insulin for every meal or drink (that's not a cucumber or water) was so painful that I became even more angry at life. Why her? Why us? Her illness made me wonder if anything I was going through at the time even compared to what she was going through.

Friends say I make diabetes look easy and I think, like most things in life, you just have to get on with it. You can only take responsibility for what you can control, and even then we are not perfect with it. As her body grows and changes naturally we also have to adjust to the internal changes too.I have Learnt along the way and just love and heal and forgive. I've hurt so many people in many ways through my own pain. At the time, I didn't even realise what I was doing, because I didn't recognise that I needed to heal from my pain, instead of using it as an excuse to hurt others. If we take the time to pay attention, a single day is full of interactions, lessons and learning opportunities. The point of this story about my daughter's diabetes, is that it made me change my perspective, my understanding and outlook about what to expect from my daily life, and how to cope with the negatives. This is where my saying,' Great Days Only', came from.

A great day doesn't have to be a perfect one. Sometimes, it's just about getting through the day regardless of what life throws at you. These days, I feel so free and happy within myself and my life that I want to share it with you so maybe you can turn your negative into a positive. That's literally a Great Day Only. But Great Days Only didn't occur to me from the get-go.

PERSPECTIVE

It took me a while to turn my negative into a positive. My daughter's health was my trigger, but I'd say that things definitely got worse before I made an active decision to make them better.

It started something like this – it was Wednesday 19th July 2015. It was the first day I'd had off work in ages and also the first week of the summer holidays. Me and my daughter had a lot of plans, from pottery painting to days out and trips around the UK and London. But before we could get on with any of these plans, we had a doctor's appointment. I managed to book the earliest appointment for 8am so that we could be in and out. Neither of us knew it at the time, but on that morning our whole life would change, and it has never been the same since. During the doctor's appointment, I mentioned that my daughter was consuming way too much water, and that no matter how much she drank, she still felt dehydrated. It felt like a strange complaint – I don't know anyone else who is concerned that their child drinks too much water. For a long time, I'd thought it was a good thing – a sign of a healthy, hydrated child. However, I started to worry when my mum said it wasn't normal for a kid to drink so much, and that it was one of the signs of diabetes.

Health

Now, at this point, I was personally 20 stone and a solid size 18-20, on the verge of Type 2 diabetes, in short Type 1 is Pancreas failure and Type 2 is Diet and Lifestyle, with my hateful height of 5'11. Though I felt I was too tall, when it came to my weight it actually served me quite well, since it meant that the extra fat was spread out more than if I'd been of average height. Even though I knew I was overweight, no one really said anything about it. Except my dad, who would out-right call me fat and tell me I needed to stop eating. As you can imagine, this wasn't helpful or encouraging - a negative punch in the fat guts. I enjoyed my food and it's not like I wasn't able to get a man. But I wasn't happy with the way I was. More on that later.

When we were called into the doctor's office, I began explaining my daughter's dehydration. I wasn't really able to think when it had started. I'd never had problems getting her to eat and drink before, so it was hard to say when I first began to notice just how much water she drank. As far as I was concerned, I was a good mum when it came to making sure my kid had a healthy diet and an active lifestyle. I made sure she took part in sports, like swimming and tennis, and 99.8% of our meals were all fresh and home cooked, including the cakes! I was proud on this front and cooked from scratch every day. The doctor pricked her finger with this small little device, which I had seen before from my grandad, who had Type 2 diabetes (diet and lifestyle). He then placed the small amount of blood onto the test strip that sits in the meter reader, which gives a blood measurement to check her sugar levels. We went through this process a couple times, as it seemed that the meter was not working as well as it should have. As it wasn't giving a clear reading, the doctor pricked her finger again, and this time was able to get a reading. The doctor looked at me and said that my daughter could have Type 1 diabetes. He sent us to the hospital immediately to have some further tests.

At this point, it's 8.04am on the first day
holidays. We were meant to be having f
go to the hospital, me reassuring her, t ....g ner it's
just a little extension to our day. We'll still get to do
all the things we planned; I tell her. On the 20-minute
car journey I don't remember thinking about anything.
I don't remember speaking. I don't remember my
daughter asking anything. Looking back, it's all just
blank. As soon as we arrived at the hospital, we were
seen immediately. The doctors rang the hospital ahead
of our arrival after I said we didn't need an ambulance.
So, there we were in the children's A&E ward. The staff
seemed to handle things well, but I didn't understand
what was happening. I felt helpless, like my daughter's
well-being was out of my control. What was supposed
to be a doctor's appointment turned into a week-long
sleep-over in the hospital ward. I can't begin to describe how I felt when she was hospitalised. My mind
went blank and I was overcome with numbness. It was
as if my mind couldn't process what was happening,
so it shut down. I felt so helpless. My baby, my only
child had a life-long condition that I couldn't do anything about (at least, not at first), and she had to endure

so much every day. The reality of it hurt my whole soul. It was a deep feeling, as if I'd been plunged into the deepest sea, adrift in a whirlwind of waves bashing against my body, ears blocked as if taking off on the runway. Writing about it has freed me a little, and I can now express with words what I used to express through anger.

Coping

One whole week passed at the hospital. During this time, I had managed to come to terms with what our new daily life was going to be like. My daughter and I were taught how to inject her insulin, and we were given guidance on the types of food to eat. We had plenty of visits from friends and family, including the man I'd loved for the past 3 years. However, the support I got from my friends and the support I got from my so-called lover was not there as I had expected. It's not like I was expecting 24/7 support, but I barely saw my partner throughout the whole of her hospitalisation. I knew something wasn't right. My intuition was rattled, a voiceless bird in a cage, sending waves of anxiety through me. I found out exactly what was wrong soon after I arrived home from the hospital, head buzzing after many sleepless nights in the ward. I was exhausted, overwhelmed with the stress of learning about the new way of life I needed to adopt to keep my daughter healthy – to keep her alive. Food and drink now had to be weighed, carb counted, and then measured for the insulin needed based on her current sugar level. Every day. Forever.

On that first evening of getting settled at home, sorting out the things I had left days ago – since the doctor's appointment – I had a phone call. My daughter was asleep so the whole house was silent. The ringing startled me, and I jumped up to answer

"Hello?"

"Yo T, you good?"

"I'm good, glad to be home."

"Ahh, you're home now, that's good."

At this moment I felt mad - not angry, mad, but strange.

PERSPECTIVE

I paused, unsure of what to say. But I had the most random weird feeling. I knew he was hiding something from me, and somehow, I knew what it was. I was silent for a moment, then I asked,

"Who's pregnant?"

The silence was everything, only answer I needed. My stomach drops. Then he says aggressively,

"Who you been talking to?"

He pauses, then says,

"Let me phone you back."

He hangs up, leaving me standing in shock in my open plan kitchen thinking, 'shit!'

This week couldn't get any worse, I thought to myself. Until it did.

It took all night to get him to say I was right. To this day, I couldn't tell you how I knew that he'd got another woman pregnant. All I can say is that I have never in my life been so in-tune with myself and my soul as I was on that night. Call it what you want, I hadn't had a conversation with anyone who knew about the pregnancy, no one had told me. I didn't know a thing until that phone call and can wholeheartedly say that it was my intuition that led me there. There is no way that I ever would have known unless he'd told me outright. My intuition is amazing, but I didn't get it 100% right. Nobody was pregnant, because the baby was already here. In the same week that my daughter was being diagnosed with Type 1 diabetes, he was at another hospital in south London with another woman while she gave birth to their child. This explained why he'd been behaving so strangely with me and not supporting me the way I expected. It's because he'd become a dad that same week.

Lying by omission

A whole nine months, and he'd not said a word to me about it. He didn't lie outright, but he didn't tell the truth either. There's actually a phrase for this: 'LYING BY OMISSION'. Lying by omission is when a person leaves out important information or fails to correct a pre-existing misconception in order to hide the truth from others. For the liar, the logic works like this; 'I didn't lie – I just didn't tell the truth'. Even though lying by omission is just as bad as lying, there are some cases where omitting the truth is not intended to be harmful and can be thought of as withholding information so as to "not hurt you". In my case, I'm convinced there was no such good intention. He wasn't protecting me; it was just convenient for him to deceive me so that I wouldn't leave or make a fuss. He was outright manipulative and toxic, bad for my mental state on a normal day – let alone after this. This was the last straw. At least, I thought it was. I was weak and I loved him. I told myself that I would never ever speak to him again let alone engage in any type of relationship with him. Oh, how wrong I was! This was about to be the ride of my life, and not in a good way. Remember, this is July 2015, the same month my daughter's life and mine had already just altered dramatically. And now this. In August 2015, I set out to Ibiza for my mum's 50th. This was a pre-planned holiday – pre-booked and paid for. This holiday couldn't have come at a better time, and still stands to date as my best holiday

– thanks ladies! Not only was it a welcome break from the troubles in my life, but it led to some important revelations that I'll say more about later. On returning from that holiday, after a lot of thought and reflection, I made an important decision: I decided to move house. I needed a new start and I needed to sort myself out. I didn't tell anyone I was moving, not my friends, not my neighbours, not anyone. It was an ongoing process from September through to December, but I moved the day before flying to Amsterdam with my childhood best friend (and bad influence) for my birthday. Even though I'd just moved house, going on a birthday trip with my friend seemed like a great idea, so off I went. While I was trying to make a fresh start for myself, I would receive messages, apologies, flowers, numerous calls. I couldn't think at the time and had found myself crying in all sorts of places and situations. I couldn't contain it. At work one day, I had to call a friend from my desk for emotional support, and I ended up having to leave the office to hyperventilate and cry my whole heart out whilst I still tried to maintain normality, I was a mess, but I contained it. Fear of allowing people at work to see me in a state forced me to control my emotions, to bottle them up. I had so many questions that I wanted answers to. However, seeking answers enabled him to be able to answer me in a way that suited his own agenda. I was weak, vulnerable, and stupid. I climbed back on the roundabout. I let him back in, but I was confused about what I wanted. I wanted him because I loved him, but I also knew that I wasn't prepared to be baby mum number two. Half the time I was convinced that I couldn't have a proper relationship with him again, not after the hurt and humiliation he'd caused me. At other times, I'd change my mind. One minute I'd be giving him the silent treatment, and the next I'd be in his arms. It was a toxic roundabout of manipulation and gas lighting. This was when I started to see the situation for what it was. I was single, but somehow, I was involved in a narcissistic relationship.

Toxicity

So, the question is, at what point do we leave toxic relationships? According to studies on Google, it takes on average a minimum of seven times for a person to leave a toxic relationship for good. What would you say your cut-off point would be? When they hit us? When they rape us? When they emotionally abuse us? Mentally abuse us? Psychologically abuse us? When they kidnap us from our own homes? Or dead lock you in their car? Hold us hostage? When they threaten the well-being of the ones around you? All true stories. What do you do when these sorts of things happen? When do you leave? Or is it just easier to conform to whatever they want to make them happy and less likely to mistreat you? When you love someone, it's natural to want to make excuses for their behaviour and to tell ourselves they don't mean it. If A wasn't happening then B and C wouldn't even be an issue, we tell ourselves. If only we can avoid triggering bad behaviour in our partners, then they won't do it again. Not only do we make these kinds of excuses for the people hurting us, but we go out of our way to protect them by lying to others about how they treat us. This can be anything from telling a friend that everything is fine, to covering up signs of physical abuse. Protecting our loved ones is a positive instinct, but not when that protection doesn't protect us also and in turn, allows them to do us harm, physical or emotional. There is also the fear that complaining or speaking out will make them mad, leading to even more hurt and pain for ourselves. But this pain is coming our way anyway, even if we keep our mouths shut. When you find yourself in this position, you need to evaluate your choices. Yes, you could stay and see what happens. Or you could leave, and see what life is like without an intimidating and/ or manipulative presence in your life. Everyone's situation may be different, but we all have choices. Even though we are sometimes faced with situations that are not ideal, not expected, and not very nice, we have a choice on how we approach them. If you are in a toxic relationship now and hoping for them to change, I hope that reading my book (or any part of it) will help you to see that it isn't just you. You are not alone. We can choose to try and work through the hurtful times in our relationships, but ask yourself, is that love? And is that what you want for forever? Some will say yes, because poor treatment is all they've known. During these difficult moments, my best advice to myself was to stay strong and keep choosing me no matter how many times I felt like I was being weak. They don't want to let you go, but they don't want to treat you right either. In some cases when we have a history of trauma, it can give us a high tolerance for emotional pain – but just because we can tolerate it, doesn't mean that we should. Its heartbreakingly hard and sad but the growth and strength that comes from that is powerful, us humans can bounce back from almost everything. I have learnt that things that hurt the most I analysed it and either repeated the cycle or I left it. The choice is ours. When do we choose us?

PERSPECTIVE

I used to have a temper

I used to have a temper
There weren't no in between
Every time I had no control
This is what we would see

One when I'm defensive
One when I feel bad
One when someone else's choice
Had made me feel so sad

This is an internal conflict
One that can't be seen
If it was on the outside
It would be all shine and gleam

It's as we ponder on the thoughts
The ones we think we know
Ones where we sit and wonder
Where did it all go?

The happiness and laughter
The tears of joy and hugs
All the meaningful connections made
That disintegrate with love

Who taught us this endeavour?
The one of life itself
Especially when we are unique
They say it can't be helped

It's all now calm and quiet
The storm has set to sea
It's so funny to sit and think that
All along the storm was me

PERSPECTIVE

Managing my weight

One good thing that came from that horrible summer of 2015, when my life and my daughter's life changed forever, is that I quickly became much more aware of what I was eating. As I mentioned earlier, my weight was a major source of unhappiness and depression for me. This isn't unusual. Fat people are often unhappy with how they look and feel. I feel like since I have body dysmorphia, I can say that. I don't mean to offend anyone, but this has been my experience. It's only now I've lost some weight that I realise I wasn't happy. I wasn't comfortable. Food and my weight used to be all I thought about, whether I was thinking about the next meal, or how I looked in whatever outfit I'd chosen to wear that day. I never felt good in clothes, and more often than not would see myself as a whale squeezed in spandex. Because of this, I hate going shopping for clothes, hated eating around other people for fear of comments. I was paranoid about the types of food I was eating and my portion sizes whenever I ate around others. I'd wonder to myself, what would I think if I saw someone my size with this plate? Carb counting did it for me, not the calories. Not the gym. The carbs.

When I realised, and understood, about carbohydrate content, I took better control of my weight. Carbohydrates are in everything, unless it's unflavoured water (which doesn't count towards your calory intake anyway) or low-carb vegetables like cucumbers. Before I was aware of carbohydrates, I didn't really think about the sorts of things I was eating. When I went to work and attended the usual morning brief, I'd have: a tea with 3 sugars: 15 carbs (equivalent to one slice of bread), a cherry Bakewell: 29.3 carbs (that's two medium slices of bread) and a jam sandwich with thick bread – it has more carbs than a single portion of lasagna. Even two slices of toast in the morning is equivalent to a lasagne (microwave portion) Still lunch, dinner and snacks to go for the rest of the day! Want to lose weight and be happier? Focus on your foods and research your carbs and start comparing what that would be in comparison to another thing. What made me start carb counting? Well, as I discussed earlier, my daughter is T1 diabetic, which means we have to weigh with scales every portion of every meal and whatever different foods she has on her plate. We also have to take note of what she eats in roughly one hour, so we can total it up. We then total the carbs based on the meal, which determines how much insulin she will need due to the amount of carbs she's consuming (the pancreas of a diabetic won't produce naturally what the body needs to process carbs). As you can imagine, going through this process on a daily basis made me much more aware of my diet and what was in it. To help my daughter avoid eating too many carbs, I had to change my diet too. Though changing your diet is difficult initially, it becomes much easier once you start getting used to healthier foods and new habits and routines.

Discipline

Why is discipline important and when do we have it?

We are all disciplined about different things. Some are disciplined to not eat and drink at the same time - which technically we shouldn't do since it interferes with digestion. Others have discipline to go to bed at a set time and also wake up at a set time - routine. Some are disciplined with food, what they eat, and how much.

Some are disciplined not to smoke or drink, not to give into peer pressure, to abstain from sex, to abstain from pleasure before doing what's needed. Sometimes we work backwards in our disciplines. I had boundaries but I didn't have the ones I needed, not when it came to eating, going to the gym, or anything to do with myself. Except work maybe - and that's a boundary I take seriously. Until procrastination kicks in. Procrastination has no boundaries, it creeps up and in without us noticing.

The little voice in our head that says other things that we can see, and others not, it tells us that when the washing up is done we will be ready, and when the cleaning is done we will be ready, and when the other things that are way less important become the more important factor then the boundary for whatever needed doing has been broken. The questions you need to ask yourself are: What areas are you disciplined in? What do you NEED to be disciplined in? What are your distractions and weaknesses? What is it you actually want so that you can embrace your new journey? When you start to be honest with yourself about these things,

PERSPECTIVE

you'll be that much closer to making positive changes in your life. It's crucial to think about the areas you're doing well in, in addition to the things that aren't going so well. For me, I knew I was pretty organised, so I found it useful to plan out my meals and activities when working towards a healthier lifestyle. In other words, I used something that I was good at to improve something I wanted to change. Use what you've already got to make an even better you!

PART 5: THE AWAKENING

It was 2015, I was 25 years old. I'd been a mum for seven years by this point, with new challenges and responsibilities. Even at the age of 25, I was completely naïve, gullible, and honestly quite angry and defensive. I was quite a negative person with negative views that often led to angry outcomes, with a roar of muted pain translated to aggressiveness. Aggression was my body's defence, preparing me for whatever was coming.

Childhood bullying

I feel like I wasn't prepared for life. As a child, I kept to myself. It was only when I started school that I really mixed with lots of other children. There were so many of them, all doing and saying so many different things. Whether they were playing games or making spiteful comments about me, they had no idea about how much their words affected me, even in later life. At this point, all I wanted was to be like everyone else. I was so sensitive. So touchy. So shy. I didn't know what life was about or what was in store for me. I didn't have a clue. Do any of us ever have a clue?

PERSPECTIVE

From a young age, I experienced bullying and criticism, though at the time this was such a normal part of my life that I wasn't even really aware of it. It was just something that happened most days and it wasn't until I was a teenager that I started reacting to it. I closed up inside, put up barriers and defences to protect myself. It would have been a trial of Fort Boyard to get through to hurt me. I was so defensive and so bent on protecting myself that I didn't even become aware of the anger growing in me. Let me paint a picture. A teenage girl, 5'10 in height, with thick glasses that magnified her eyes, UK Size 9 size feet, frizzy hair, and special dentistry required (my mouth wasn't big enough for all my teeth, so they overlapped). I felt different – something that wasn't helped by my mixed-race skin colour, which made me stand out even more. I would often think to myself, who the fuck am I and where did I come from? Why am I so different and what on earth is going on?

These questions plagued me endlessly. And it wasn't just me thinking them. Other kids commented on my appearance, saying things like: Look at her shoes! Why are your feet so big? Why are you so tall? Why are your glasses like that – they're like magnifying glasses! I remember someone snatching my glasses from my face and doing a couple of laps around the classroom while everyone laughed. That classroom became for me like Harry Potter's room under the stairs – so small, so tiny, so hidden. Not that I could see much of what was going on anyway. That kid was running around with my vision. Literally.

Breaking down barriers

I didn't even know all of this affected me until I was an adult. It was during my first lot of CBT (cognitive behaviour therapy) session and I was asked if I had ever been bullied. I was immediately on the defence. How could someone bully *me*? I'm sure I even had a little laugh at the mere thought of it. Whenever I didn't like what was being said or done, I'd create such a scene that no one would even want to attempt to have anything to say to me. I thought briefly for a second, looking back on all those confrontations. I realised I never actually placed any of the situations I'd encountered as bullying. I felt like acceptance of bullying made me some kind of weak victim. My ego could never let this happen. But putting my ego away for a bit made me understand that me being this way wasn't actually me! It was a 'me' I created to protect the real me. The sensitive me. The caring me. The thoughtful me, the loving me. The happy me. I had been hidden. By myself. For myself. Hidden from a world where I expected everyone to be like me, and to care about how I presented myself. Because that's all we really know in our minds – ourselves – to the point that even now, I sometimes push people away, automatically guarding myself from them. In part, my defensive reactions depend on the energy other people bring with them. But I also know that my reactions are to do with me, and my fears about others hurting me. Life experiences will have you doing this sort of thing – building barriers and defences. I suppose it's different for everyone, depending on what sort of person they are, and what they've individually experienced. This is why there is no book of life. There's no one way to cope with things, no one way to heal. The journey to self-love is different for each of us, but it starts with self-awareness, with recognising who you are and why you are the way you are. For a long time, I didn't really have self-awareness. This is something I developed later in life, when I started to realise how broken I'd become. When you realise that something is wrong, that your life isn't what you think it should be, that's when we have to search. Why are we the way we are? Why do we behave in certain ways? Now, I'm no behavioural specialist, but I can most definitely see that my behaviour wasn't normal, that it came from a place of self-hate. It wasn't until I was an adult having CBT that I realised I had been a victim of bullying. Admitting this to myself was an important step in gaining self-awareness.

PERSPECTIVE

<u>Thoughts</u>

I've got loads of questions
Running 'round my head
Way too many in there
I can't put them to bed

Even when I'm sleeping
Sometimes in a dream
They can be so vivid
Except not what it seems

My mind has all these memories
From when I learned to think
To keep them nice and organised
OCD at its brink

So, now they sit in storage
And when I take them out
I lose all track of everything
Then in creeps the doubt

I opened up the wrong one
Now all I do is think
The dreams more of a nightmare now
The thoughts are at its brink

The thoughts have taken over
Like knots all in our hair
The tangles got us caught up
My eyes all in a glare

I'm going through the boxes
If even one by one
You'll feel the sense of healing
As you untangle the bun

So, sit back and relax
It's not about what's more
Surely ask your thoughts
And they can show you to the door

The door is small and simple
An entrance to our brain
Something to remember
For when I come back again

My thoughts are contradicting
There're voices in my head
One or two I have no clue
I just hear what it had said

PERSPECTIVE

It told me that I'm worthy
It told me not to run
It told me when I can't take no more
To go and find some fun

Go and be so happy
Free as thoughts can be
You don't have to stay in one place
For you are not a tree

This life has many lessons
So, listen to your thoughts
Don't try to derail them
This is your train of thought

Make sure that it's respectful
Make sure that it's clean
Even for a child's ears
There's nothing in between

So, take this happy moment
And make it last all day
It's not our thoughts that control us
It's also what we say

When you speak, it is power
Magic written in the walls
If only you could see it
You wouldn't make certain calls

Not only on the phone
But just in life itself
It's only when we take this time
We realise it affects our wealth

Our wealth not as in money
Or things that we can see
But in the way we know and feel
It's complementary

So, take yourself away
and have a little pause
You might want to sit and think
And close some of the doors

For doors that will stay open
Welcome in the past
But this is not a roundabout
For sure you'll fall off fast.

PERSPECTIVE

Understanding intent

It's important to be aware of who we have in our space. Our energy has to be preserved for what matters and who matters. I personally have had too many occasions where I've been manipulated into doing what other people want or think. Rather than thinking for myself. But when you spend any amount of time with a person or group of people, you start to conform to their expectations and behaviours. I've been in the presence of many narcissistic individuals (male and female) and it takes a strong person to overcome those challenging situations and scenarios. Especially when you're not confident in yourself or in your judgement. It was a gradual process for me, and it took multiple situations and scenarios for me to develop an understanding of what didn't sit right with my spirit.

My brain and spirit and aura will auto detect for everything these days. I can feel a bad vibe a mile away. When I start sensing that someone is pushing me towards a course of action I don't want to take, or towards a frame of mind I don't want to be in, I start asking myself these questions? Who are they, and what do they want from me? What's their motive and intention? When we pick up the phone and dial a number to call - that's calling with intention. When we feel hungry and we make plans and arrangements to eat - that's also with intention. jump in the car – yeah you get my drift. Everything that we face in life follows the same basic pattern: choice, decision, intention, and effect (which may not match our original intention). So, when women are approached by men, at what age do we become aware that their intention isn't usually to get to know us and have a long-lasting friendship? It's different for all of us; some girls are aware of male attention and the intent behind it from a young age, while others might not understand the attention they receive until well into adulthood. Typically, however, this is something that girls start to think about in their teens. I'm not for one moment suggesting that whenever men speak to us, they have ulterior motives. But at the same time, we can't assume that everyone has pure intentions. If this was the case, we would trust and love everyone and have no worries in the world. Unfortunately, we can't afford to fully trust. We have to look after ourselves and our interests, and in fact most of us do this on a daily

PERSPECTIVE

basis without even realising. For example: Why do we lock our car? Why do we lock our home? Why do we insure our things? Because not everyone has the same good intentions that we do. And we could fall victim to what is seen as an opportunity. Although it's quite easy to protect ourselves from obviously bad intentions (like people who might want to steal our cars and TV's, etc.), it's less easy to protect ourselves from people who pretend to have good intentions. This might be a stranger, a significant other, or a close family member. These days, I don't let other people's intentions affect me in a negative way. For a long time though, I thought I was successfully fending-off bad intentions by changing who I was – by becoming a more aggressive version of my kind, quiet, compassionate self. I felt that I had to be angry to protect myself, as mad as that may sound. I became a bitch. I went from someone who would do anything and everything for the people I loved, to someone who became hostile and defensive. I thought that I was protecting myself, but actually I was changing myself – allowing myself to become a worse person because of the way others behaved towards me. Now that I'm aware of this, I try to avoid coming across as confrontational, and to pay attention to my own responses. The message is: don't let other people's intentions control you. When you understand their intentions, you can control your responses, and act in the best way for YOU.

Reactions vs responses

Every day is a different battle; make a choice in all you do. Decide how you react. Furthermore, don't react. Respond. Reactions are instantaneous – it just isn't possible to think them out. Responses are deliberate and considered. Responses put you in control. Other people won't ever completely understand you (even when they think they do). We know what's what with ourselves, right? Are you true to your feelings or do you cut them off and block them out and seek temporary distractions? Do you prefer to stay in the safety of the past, repeating past behaviour and mixing with the same people instead of moving on to better things? If we stay in our comfort zones then we stay in the same place. There's a great book actually relating perfectly to this. It is called 'Who Moved My Cheese' by

PERSPECTIVE

Spencer Johnson. Johnson wrote a short book that explores how and why we should address change in our lives. Cheese is a metaphor for "What we want in life", whether that be in personal or professional circumstances. The one constant we have in life is change. "If we do not change, we can become extinct" and "the quicker we let go of old cheese the sooner we find new cheese". When cheese goes off, it smells, so keep your sense of smell on alert. This is a compelling fable on the importance of keeping 'change' as a way of life and assent to its core principles. We can relate to the mice since there are choices and decisions to be made. We can either be a bum with a lousy job, lousy friends, lousy bank accounts, no man that sticks around, nothing great really happening. Just a daily, weekly, monthly, yearly repetition of the same old thing! You see, when you don't work on yourself (which at times I don't), that has a domino effect. But by becoming more aware daily, weekly, and monthly, I am becoming a master of myself. The last five years have definitely been unbelievably stressful to say the least, with hurt causing an unexpected transition. It was a lonely process. But sometimes, something has to happen to get you to that point where change is a stand, a refusal to accept your current situation. You are worthy. I can tell you this, but can *you* tell me you are? We can place our hand on our heart, but it doesn't mean we have found self-love. It means we are alive, but it doesn't mean we're getting the most out of life. We can stand and say that we love ourselves and who we are but saying isn't the same as doing. Saying 'I love myself' is quick and easy, whereas doing what it takes to truly develop self-love is harder and longer, but ultimately far, far more effective than mere words.

The mask

Most of us wear a mask that tells the rest of the world that we're ok, that we're winning at life. We wear these masks for so long that we forget we're wearing them. To hide your troubles from behind a mask is heart-breaking when you are broken. You can't see behind anyone else's mask, so you don't know where to turn for empathy and support. It can feel very lonely. We can't love ourselves while we wear that mask. We have to look honestly at what's behind it, at our true selves. It's not about the confident ones, the ones who dress well, speak well, or even say that they love themselves, and act like it to the point of self-obsession. I can't say for certain if outwardly confident people are really, honestly confident, or if it's just an act – their way of putting up a defence against the world. Whatever the case, self-love isn't about showing off or impressing others. It's about accepting ourselves for who we are and allowing ourselves to make choices about our happiness.

Love can bring out the best in us. The strength to be confident and move on. The courage to be truthful. The strength to be hopeful. But this love can't come exclusively from other people; it has to come from within you too. These days, I don't feel the need to retaliate when someone hurts or annoys me. I literally wish them all the best and eliminate them from my life. It's a privilege to be a part of my life and my energy. Not because of my job, my books, my other business ventures, my financial status, relationship status or even because you think I think I'm better than anyone. This is never and will never be the case. It's because

I'm a lover and a giver. And as much as I'm nice, I can also not be nice. a lot of the time, peoples projections are them exposing how unhappy they are, but may not even be aware of it. I may make a joke out of it or be so nice that whoever intended to hurt or annoy me will peel away, revealing their true selves while I remain in control of mine.

As soon as you lose it, you've lost control. This is something that motherhood in particular has taught me! I'm not interested in confrontation or what other people think of me. I walk around with a smile. I like smiling at people. I love laughing. I like making others smile. I like helping others find 'their happy state', I like being happy. I like being calm and relaxed. I love passionate conversations – not with people who think I'm arguing though. I enjoy the company of people. But not too much. I'm a sensitive soul and can only take so much energy at one time. I don't provoke others intentionally, even if they're the ones trying to get a reaction from me. I'm not saying I never have! Oh, I'm sure we all have our stories or breakdowns, maybe both. But in my recent years of learning, I realised that getting myself out of overwhelming situations is my responsibility. How I treated myself and others was definitely a turning point for me. Knowing when to unleash your inner beast and when to keep it tamed is key when dealing with difficult people. But I also won't be bullied, with everything there are boundaries. My boundaries are important – so might be a sting to push it – do so at your own risk.

Shame vs embarrassment

Me and my sister, Mina, were talking one day about embarrassment. Now, Mina is very expressive, as am I. But we differ in our forms of expression. Mina is my younger sister on my mum's side, and I'd say we are pretty close. She taught me that it's important to be yourself. This wasn't a lesson she taught me in one day. It's something I'd watched over a period of years while observing her growing up. I found (and still find) her hilarious. Crying and belly hurting hilarious. Telepathic conversations. Understand a face expression and laugh till the cows come home. Be in stitches about the silliest of things. We have a great connection. She's my soul best friend. Mina's real-life character is very genuine. She can go from being a bit blonde to coming out with the most random fact in the world, from being ditzy to being a businesswoman. Her journey at a young age in what she does and who she is, is a story in itself. She found a video of something one day that said something along the lines of: 'You're only embarrassed if you let yourself feel shame towards a given situation. You control you. Sometimes we can act out of character based on the embarrassment we feel at the time. Whereas if you don't care, and you don't feel anything towards it, then you don't feel embarrassed.' WOAH! Being genuine can sometimes mean opening yourself up to embarrassment. But this advice Mina had found seemed to be saying that embarrassment itself was a choice. It comes from shame, and shame is something we can control. This advice could apply to all sorts of different situations. For example, it might be that you find yourself at a restaurant with a meal that hasn't been cooked properly so you send it back. Not in a rude way, but the dish gets sent back and a new one is made and brought to you. Now, let's say the person at the table with you crumbles with shame over your complaint. Their shame infects you, spoiling the whole evening, over what is actually a very small incident. Reflecting on the incident and realising it isn't a cause for shame removes embarrassment, and therefore negativity. One of the really negative things about shame is that it can change your behaviour. For example, feeling shame over a dish that you sent back is likely to discourage you from doing the same thing again, which means you've primed yourself to accept low quality for fear of 'making a scene' and embarrassing yourself and others. In other words, shame can stop us from being assertive, whether in terms of speaking up when you see something wrong or making a simple request. Another common cause of social embarrassment can come from being loud and laughing in places where it's quiet. When I socialise with friends and family, I can completely block out my surroundings and just focus on the fun I'm having, on whatever's making me laugh or making me happy. I don't worry about being louder than the people around me, because I'm just not aware of anyone outside my social unit. They don't control my enjoyment or my reactions. This makes me free of embarrassment to an extent because I don't care about what other people think. And that's it! That's what it's all about. Embarrassment is what you feel in regard to what you ASSUME SOMEONE ELSE THINKS. ASS U ME (assume). Don't make an arse of you and me. The more comfortable we are within ourselves, the better it is for us in all traits we hold.

PERSPECTIVE

Sometimes I feel like writing

Sometimes I feel like writing
It softens out the pain
To get some of his old hurt out
It's like it flows all down the drain

The hurt that isn't spoken
For no-one understands
It's like when you're on the beach
And full body under sand

It's soft but also heavy
It don't come all at once
To even build a sandcastle
You need it like some mud

The texture keeps it stuck there
Like memories we replay
It's only when I feel like this
The words they come and stay

So, write them down and keep them
memories in the rain
The little thoughts that make us think
About you once again

In life it's just our memories
The ones that make you smile
You have to heal
And forgive a bit
To keep your sacred smile

So, live your life so freely
With memories at your feet
It's only when you look back 'round
It's like looking through the sleet.

The sleet's as thick as raindrops
Falling from the clouds
It's what made my vision blur
It's like a big huge crowd

The present moment's priceless
It gives you what you see
It's only when I realised this
I realised I was blind to me

PERSPECTIVE

<u>Ibiza Mornings</u>

This was a much-needed break, to say the least. I explained earlier in the book how the summer of 2015 was shaping up to be a terrible time in my life. Firstly, because of the news that my daughter had Type 1 diabetes, and secondly because I'd discovered that my partner at the time had just had a baby with another woman. The year that I'd had! And we were only in August. I needed this holiday, more than I even knew. It was the last day on a beautiful island. My mum, aunt, and sister were off to JET apartments to have one more dance off (email me for the video that went viral on Facebook). After a few days of pumping music, people, and heavy drinking, I decided the last day was only for chilling. Me and my mum's friend sat in the sand at the back entrance of our hotel on the beach, with our drink and smoke in hand. We spoke about all kinds of different things. But the one thing that stayed with me since is this:

In the sand, she drew with her finger 'me' and placed a large circle around it.

At this point, she had my full attention.

She said, no matter what happens in life, or who comes at you in your circle, ◯

you have a choice about whether or not you let them get inside your circle.

You can let in whoever you want — friends, family, people you care about. But if they become a toxic presence in your life, you can push them back out. You control your circle.

PERSPECTIVE

The bottom line is, nothing can get inside unless you allow it. I should create a better drawing of this like the mind map. My mind was officially blown. And we just sat at the seashore and watched the waves come in with the indecent sound of the party life circulating all around us. I was only there physically. My mind was completely in a state of shock. I'll always remember that day – that simple drawing in the sand the changed the way I viewed myself and my life forever.

PART 6: MANAGING OUR EXPECTATIONS

It's a scary time to be in the world. Single or in a relationship. I've had many conversations with individuals from all kinds of backgrounds and experiences, from lesbians and gay couples to people in open relationships. If there's one thing I've learnt, it's that no type of relationship is immune to becoming toxic.

Earlier this year I interviewed some couples and also some single people, and asked them what they wanted from a relationship. We all say some unrealistic things, or things that we can't actually reciprocate. These were some of the answers:

Treats us well

Buys us things

Surprises us

Owns a car

Lives alone

Earns great money

PERSPECTIVE

Since nobody's perfect, we have to think about what's most important to us when it comes to choosing a man. For example, is it ok if he treats us great but has no job? Or, is bad treatment acceptable if the sex is good or if we're getting gifts to make up for the bad stuff? Then there are things we all know we definitely don't want: no cheating; no crazy baby mammas; no crazy ex or side chick coming to vandalise our cars; no violent or aggressive behaviour. But it's not enough to only think about what we expect from them. The questions we really have to ask ourselves are, do we know who we are, what we like, and what makes us happy? If we don't know these things, and don't communicate these things, then we can't expect others to know how to make us happy and feel good about ourselves. We get upset when they don't seem to know us, but do WE know US?

All I wanted from a relationship was a man who focused on working towards his goals while giving me – and only me – 100% of his interest. If he's the right guy, you know in a short space of time that it's working. A decent man is consistent with himself and with you.

PART 6: MANAGING OUR EXPECTATIONS

He has aspirations and takes pride in his work. If he's a dad, he's a good dad, and does whatever it takes to look after his children. If this is you, salute! Bravo! Honestly, it's lovely to see. Of course, not all men are like this. Those who aren't able to offer emotional stability to their partners and children need to find a way to help themselves. Because that's where it starts. Help yourself to heal and helping others will follow. Often, we expect the men/women in our lives to do for us what they can't do for themselves. We expect love, support, and respect, but not everyone is capable of giving us those things. You don't necessarily have to love yourself to love others, but if you don't at least have self-respect, then it's unlikely that you'll be able to show proper respect in a relationship. Self-hate breeds hateful relationships. This isn't always the case, but it's something I've experienced, and I've had many conversations that all led back to this.

Many men that I have spoken to this year, say that they want a loyal woman. A woman who doesn't even put herself in the position of temptation, who has self-control. A woman who looks after her family, her household and her business. A woman who strives for more in life to keep up with herself. An independent woman who doesn't need a man but wants a partner. A person. Their person. But the question is, can you replicate what you require? Can you be all those things you want your partner to be? Understanding what you want from a relationship will help you make good decisions on choosing a partner and knowing when it's time to leave. When deciding if a man is right for you, it's also important to find out about them and how they grew up. What have their experiences been, and how might this affect how they behave towards you? As a child, did they learn how to cook and clean? There are all kinds of upbringings, and we can't control everything about how we're raised. But we can learn from it.

One important thing to remember is that YOU set the bar for how your partner treats you. How you treat yourself will affect how they treat you. These are some of the questions I started asking myself:

Do I reject my own feelings to accept someone else?

Do I ignore (neglect) my own needs or want to give someone else theirs?

PART 6: MANAGING OUR EXPECTATIONS

Do I abuse myself in a way that affects me and others? (sometimes without even being aware).

If you answer yes to any of these questions, that suggests you need to change how you think about yourself. Then you can decide what sort of treatment you're prepared to accept. Some people act like you have to give up part of yourself when you begin a relationship. The phrase 'falling for someone' implies just that – that you've given something up in order to be with someone else. Let's stop falling for people and let's stand by each other's side. Be each other's 100%.

All my life, I've heard the expression "this is my other half". Other half meaning that they are not a whole. I want to be a whole – a full 100% within myself.

I come with my 100%, you come with your 100%. We now have 200%, we are winning! When I'm having a bad day, and I'm down 10% to 90%, fill me with 5%.

If you want someone to be there for you 100%, then you have to be there for them 100%. And in order to be a whole person, you have to find happiness within yourself by figuring out what makes you happy. If you can't find a way to do this, you'll always be reliant on your partner to fill up your 'other half'.

Parenting: reality vs posing

Healthy relationships are important, because children often emulate the behaviour of their parents. Your input matters. Every part of it. I'm not a perfect mum. I even struggle to say I'm a good one. My daughter would say different. She keeps me going. No parent is perfect. We're learning too, just like our children. Trying to be a good mum is the hardest ongoing thing I've encountered in this life, but also the most rewarding. Every time she's a year older there's a whole bundle of things that come with it, things that I've never experienced. It's my first time doing it all! I wasn't given a handbook! I was given a red book for 'Jabs log' and brochures on how to stay healthy with their flu jabs. Parenting has been a huge learning curve for me and deserves a book all to itself. But all parents, or mums-to-be for the first, second, or third-plus time, will say it's different with them all. Everything. The pregnancy, the cravings, the birth. Sometimes even the dads! None of us were handed a leaflet to tell us what to expect and what to do. We are human. We make mistakes and I think it's great for kids to see that. It's also important for our kids to see how we rectify our mistakes, and how we learn from them. Taking ownership and accountability for our mistakes is crucial. This means apologising when we are wrong and correcting the things we have done as best as we can. Who we have our children with is very important? If your partner is not consistent, loving, and supportive, then chances are they won't magically turn into any of these things when they become a parent. At the same time, the way your partner behaves towards you doesn't necessarily reflect how they'll behave with a child. In order to decide if you want to have children with someone, it's a good idea to test them a little. Now, I don't mean drastic stuff. All I mean is, become a little more observant. See how they behave around your friends' kids and your family's kids. Not everyone is great with children from the get-go, but you can definitely get an impression of the type of parent someone might turn out to be based on how they deal with the children already in both of your lives. Are they patient with kids? Are they kind? Do they ignore them, or speak sharply without cause? All of these things are worth paying attention to. Of course, parenting skills come with time and practice, and most people find things are different when it comes to their own child. Not everyone has maternal or paternal instincts, but this doesn't mean they will never develop them. However, if you have serious doubts about a partner, then know this: you can't make someone a dad by making them a dad. That comes from them, from who they are. How they were raised, what standards and morals they have. Some people are only parents socially. 'What do I mean by this?' you may be asking. Well, it seems to me that some people are only parenting on social media, updating the world on their child's success at school, while ignoring the negative things. It might be, for example, that a child does well at school, but has terrible manners and behaviours at home. You can be proud of your child without constantly boasting on social media. In any case, most of this bragging is more about parents showing off their parenting skills than it is about the well-being of their children. I'm immensely proud of my daughter, but I prefer to focus on my interactions with her rather than posting stuff on social media to all my friends. Honestly, I could scream when I see some stuff people post!

Support and encouragement

Support doesn't necessarily mean paying for everything, which could make us become dependent, and which can also be a form of control. To some, giving time is more important than giving gifts. If your partner makes time for you when he's busy in order to offer you help and support, he's the sort of man you should keep in your life. Support means giving you encouragement and listening to you – not just pretending to! Support means giving comfort, love, and affection. Throwing money at a relationship is never a good thing, and you should be wary of men who use money as a substitute for other things, unless this makes you happy and content . I now think a relationship requires regular maintenance, just like a seed we plant in the hope that it will grow into something healthy and wholesome. Invest time and care, and you'll reap the rewards. Talking to plants has been shown to make them happier, and this goes for relationships too! Talk to your partner. If you ignore or neglect them, your relationship will suffer. All of this seems obvious, but one of the biggest complaints among couples is that their partner doesn't listen to them or spend enough time with them. We know the advice, but we don't always abide by it.

Plants are prone to attack from outside forces, like bugs and parasites. Sometimes you have to fight off these attacks to protect the relationship. It's not always obvious when an external factor works its way into your relationship with negative results. This could be an affair, trouble at work, or family issues – the possibilities are endless. Being aware of these sorts of things without obsessing over them can feel like a tricky balancing act, and we don't always get it right. In fact, burying your head in the sand or going crazy with paranoia can often seem easier than dealing with the grey area in between. When it comes to relationships, you can't rely on your partner to feel good about yourself. They should definitely boost your confidence, but you need to draw on inner confidence too. This is where personal care comes in. Do whatever you need to do in order to feel good about yourself, whether this involves stepping fresh out of the shower, putting on a bit of make-up, getting your hair done, or treating yourself to a brand-new outfit. 'Letting yourself go' is a phrase we often hear. It sounds quite nasty, but what people tend to mean when they say this is 'don't give up on yourself', 'don't lose confidence'. Feeling good about yourself is good for you, and for your relationship. That goes for both men and women!

Setting an example

I mentioned earlier that kids learn their behaviours from their parents. If you have a strong relationship, chances are your child will learn how to develop these too. But what if you come from a broken home? What if the only relationships you were exposed to as a kid were negative ones? Does this mean you can't be a good parent? Of course it doesn't! The key is to learn from those negative relationships. First, acknowledging what made them bad. How did you feel about them at the time? Understanding the causes behind those negative relationships will help you from repeating any mistakes you may have witnessed in your childhood. If you are able to, talk to your parents and loved ones about those early experiences. Try to understand and learn from them. I think in these sections we should have it as the definitions – this is the thing I've spoken about it but it's in knowing what it actually is – not everyone can relate to one story but can relate to exactly what something means – and not from my opinion but from what it is. What values has your childhood instilled in you that impact your tolerance levels in relationships? For example, how did you view relationships at a young age? What were they, who had them, and how did they behave? The relationships that are likely to have had the biggest impact on you are your parents', whether they were together or with other partners. We also learn about relationships from other family members, such as grandparents, aunts and uncles, and older siblings. When thinking about the behaviour of particular couples, consider the following questions: Did the couple argue? Did they fight? Were they happy, distant, did they lie to each other? Were you a 24/7 witness to that relationship? Did you ever question whether the relationship was a good or bad one? Did your parents leave you, care for you? Were you aware of cheating? Did you hear conversations that your mind couldn't even really understand or comprehend? As a parent myself, I've asked myself these questions to gain more understanding about relationships and how they've affected me. By understanding the way I think and feel about relationships, and how my perceptions have changed over the years, I have more of an insight into how my daughter might think about and develop relationships. I want her understanding to be better than mine, want her to expect and demand more than I did. This is something she has to learn for herself, but also from the role models in her life. We can't want more if we don't know there's more out there to find. Sometimes we need someone to show us.

PART 7: PRESSURE AND MANIPULATION

The poisoned apple

The story of Snow White is a great analogy for pressure and manipulation. She's tricked into accepting an apple from a witch disguised as a poor old woman. The witch lures her in when she is vulnerable and alone. Snow White doesn't really want the apple, but she's pressured into taking one and biting into it then and there.

What is on offer isn't actually wanted, or even being looked for, but is still being offered, declined politely, and rejected repeatedly. Through a combination of force and guilt, Snow White is made to feel as if she has to take the apple, so she does. Pressure comes in many forms of disguise. Let's change it up and paint a different picture. What if the witch in the story was actually an older man who was pressurising a young lady to eat an apple? When Snow White declines, the man continues to pressure her and refuses to leave her alone until she complies. This would change how we perceived the situation, since an older man is a much more obvious threat to a young girl than a poor old woman is. Perceiving threats isn't always easy, so we have to be careful about who we trust. I believe we are manipulated all the time, every day for many, many things that we aren't even aware of. How many of us just go with the flow of what everyone else wants or suggests, whether it's our phones checking what we search and providing us with buying options left, right, and centre, or people we believe to be genuine who use and abuse our trust. How do we recognise pressure and manipulation for what they are? Sometimes we can recognise these things internally, based on what we ourselves are experiencing. At other times, we might recognise it happening to other people, from an external perspective.

The drone effect

Gaining an external perspective on the things going on in my life is something I refer to as the 'drone effect'. I like to visualise it as if I am in google maps and the destination is me, then remotely zoom out of my current surroundings and see everything from a bird's eye view to gain a different perspective.

When presented in any situation or circumstance, we have a choice 98.9% of the time. Everything is a choice. Being in certain types of situations used to make me feel under pressure. I'd often feel as though I had to give an immediate answer or react or respond on the spot. Deciding when to make a decision is also a choice. We can say, 'can I have a moment?' in order to give ourselves space to process whatever decision we are faced with. In some instances, we don't have to respond at all. We literally have the choice and power to do and choose what we want (within reason!). From today, be aware that you have a choice in everything you do and say. Be aware that you have a voice. Communication became a great tool for me. Rather than expressing frustration or negativity towards a situation, I would just express what I thought. I might have to adjust my thoughts at times, so they don't come across rude, but honest reactions are important. It gave me great freedom to just be honest in what I choose.

PART 7: PRESSURE AND MANIPULATION

Re-evaluating happiness: perception vs reality

Sometimes we accept unhappiness, believing that it will transform into happiness eventually. This is often the reason that so many people stay in unhappy, abusive relationships. They see light at the end of the tunnel, which prevents them from making a big change in their lives. Change can be frightening, especially when it comes to the big stuff, like jobs and relationships. We tend to think that the 'known' is a safer place to be than the unknown. Likewise, we associate relationships with happiness and protection, and the absence of relationships with loneliness and unhappiness. But what happens when those relationships turn unhappy? Do we cling to them for fear of being alone? Or do we explore what makes us happy without a partner in our lives? The first choice might seem easier, but it can present many more difficulties than embracing a change in the long term. Sometimes we can be so deeply enmeshed in a bad relationship that we don't even realise we have a choice to leave. This is where self-awareness comes in. In order to recognise the option for change, we need to honestly assess our emotional state. We see people around us that seem happy. This can sometimes make us feel like we're not normal if we're not happy too. But it's important to remember that displays of happiness are often for show. Just because a couple seems happy in public or on social media, doesn't mean that everything about their relationship is great. In fact, things could be terrible. We just don't know. That being the case, judging the strength of our relationships based on how other people present theirs isn't the best idea. Public personas often don't match what's going on inside or in private. We show off, we portray a sense of fulfilment within ourselves, we lie to others and say small statements like 'I'm really good', 'things are going well', 'I'm happy', and 'we're happy'. We only show our true selves to a select few, people we can trust to show us empathy and support when things aren't ok. It's a vulnerable place to be. You can't speak to everyone about everything. Good or bad. The phrase, it's 'A Cinderella Story', is something we often hear, but rarely experience for ourselves: a beautiful girl meets prince charming, and they live happily ever after. Who wouldn't want this?! The trouble is, if we have expectations that we're going to be like Cinderella - the perfect story - we are going to be very disappointed. Furthermore, if we really look at Cinderella, we only see a perfect snapshot of her life. Her 'happily ever after' occurred in her teens. We're told that she lived happily ever after, but we don't see it. We see only what the storyteller wants us to see. For anyone who has seen happy couples posting pictures of themselves on social media, this probably sounds quite familiar! They are storytellers, showing those aspects of their relationship that they want us to see. Everything else remains hidden. On the other hand, some people prefer to keep their relationships completely private. In these cases, it's easy to believe that they are the happiest couple going. We might even look up to them as role-models for the perfect relationship, using them for our own 'couple goals'. They may display public affection now and then (keeping up appearances so others don't question the perfect), but they keep their relationship private. This doesn't necessarily mean that anything is wrong; some people are generally private by nature. But imagine if things weren't kept so private, that we did talk about heartbreak and hurt. Imagine if we were open and honest about what to avoid, what

PERSPECTIVE

not to accept and what not even to tolerate. 'Each one, teach one'. What if we shared our relationship difficulties without judgement and without prejudice? I think this would lead to much healthier relationships, since there would be less focus on ideals and more focus on reality. If people were honest about their relationships, we would gain a more realistic perspective. The story might go something like this: One imperfect guy meets an imperfect girl. They get together based on a mix of different things – interests, likes, physical attraction. Their lives play out like everyone else's, with ups and downs, obstacles and achievements, joy and pain. Whether or not they stay together depends on both of their choices as they move through life.

No one is perfect – it's not a movie, or a fairy-tale. It's real life. We all have flaws, but as a couple you get through it together.

Entertainment vs pleasure

When I say, 'entertainment versus pleasure', I'm talking about the entertainment that temporarily holds our attention, rather than pleasure, which comes from intentionally doing things that make us happy. Entertainment is incidental and can be used to distract us from true happiness and pleasure – nothing more, nothing less.

Charm and manipulation

Charm seems like such a nice, positive word. It conjures images of perfection, like Prince Charming. The word 'charming' is used to describe good behaviour, and to describe people we perceive as good: 'A charming young lady', or 'A charming young man', we might say, to show our approval. But what is charm, and how do people use it to their advantage?

Charm can easily turn into manipulation, and we need to be careful about the effects of 'charm' on our interactions with others. First, let's find out what it is and how it works in an example below. Charmers fade into the background as they make their target the centre of attention. They listen and observe but give little away about themselves. The thing is, unless you are a narcissist or a charmer and manipulator, then you don't know the behaviour that would be a red flag until you're being manipulated. A charmer lets their target talk and reveal themselves. The more they talk, the more they reveal. A charmer wants to find out the strengths and weaknesses of their target and use these to their advantage to charm and manipulate them further. They pay you compliments and do things that mimic your behaviour and opinions, making it feel like you have so much in common yet they're just trying to get past your barriers. You are left feeling heard and understood. You're grateful to them for paying so much attention, for listening so sincerely. This can also be labelled as gaslighting.

By adapting to the emotions of their target, the charmer is able to draw out sadness, worries, strengths, and abilities. They are able to access your whole story and journey. They will use this to massage your ego, making you feel good about yourself. But to what end? That's the question you must ask whenever you notice this happening. The charmer will also encourage the worst in you, letting you spill out all those negatives, which become weapons for the charmer. At this point, they almost have you. If the charmer does their work well, they will make you into a circus monkey, performing whenever they tell you to. In other words, you'll become dependent on the charmer. Charmers make gestures of self-sacrifice, no matter how fake it may seem. They do this to show their target how much they care and how much they're willing to sacrifice. Charmers offer obvious sources of pleasure, but rarely offer anything that is more than skin deep. They'll distract you with fun, frivolous activities, making themselves seem generous and spontaneous – holidays, adventures, shopping trips. This is the ultimate charmer: or also known as, 'the buyer'. This might sound brilliant, but someone who can potentially make you financially dependent upon them whilst in the 'charm state' can be dangerous. This is where we can get lost in the charm. Lost in the manipulation. This is a recipe for a bad cake. How long do we continue when on every page of that recipe book there is a yellow flag? The decided recipe (choice/awareness) is definitely multiple red flags. In the chance that you encounter those who are closed-off or aggressive, you should back off. Let them have their little victories. These people usually have no control over themselves and are likely to be naturally aggressive/defensive.

Conspiracy #ThePlan

The charmer knows how to smooth out any conflict - see the first syllable 'CON'. They are never obviously negative or directly rude. They know that this will enhance your defence mode, making you less susceptible to their charm. Instead of direct confrontation, they'll use subtler methods of getting what they want from you. They'll plant ideas, hint and suggest stuff. Because you are charmed, you'll find yourself wanting to do what they suggest. Unaware of the power they have over you, you're becoming increasingly weak and vulnerable, without even realising it. You're lured in, thinking that you're loved when in fact you are being used. This unknown sorcery isn't taught in your usual school studies. Now that we know what a charmer is and how they behave, how many of us can say we've been the target of a charmer, that we've been completely manipulated without even being aware of it?

They might not have even been aware of it. Habits and behaviours and experience got them there. *They* might not actually see themselves as charmers. Or they might hide behind other words, like 'charismatic', or 'extrovert'. It's a different story for all charmers, but their motives and results tend to be pretty similar: gaining control over someone else. How many of us are really aware of what we are experiencing? If we are the sum of our experiences, how can we even begin to step out of ourselves and gain a different perspective about what's going on? This last heartbreak of mine hurt me so much that I questioned EVERYTHING. Painful as it was, it's definitely paid off – not just in life lessons, but also in financial success. Everything we said we would achieve together, I've achieved on my own. Hopefully you'll be aware of charm after reading this. You might even find you can use it to your own advantage in gaining self-awareness.

PERSPECTIVE

Distant reflections

When you give me this distance
It makes me self-reflect
Who have I been all along
And do I stand correct?

It made me question lots of things
Including am I worthy
Except when I see it now
Are YOU even sturdy?

Strong enough to hold me
Like I do when you're weak
To stand and support everything
Is motivation at its peak

You say I'm a strong woman
One who holds her own
Except when you came to pick me up
You threw me like a stone

Now I am here just wondering
What made you let me go
With so much distance between us
My heart's as cold as snow

Having me was such a blessing
You shouldn't have left so soon
Those seeds we would have planted
Would soon be in full bloom

We have to tend to the plants
Love them and help them grow
Give them what they need so they can
Give us what we sow

This is a real-life story
It happens all the time
This is just a glimpse
Of a chapter which is mine

I give it back in gratitude
Said thanks and let it go
I loved what it had taught me
The soil made me grow

I didn't want to leave you
But your distance made me sad
I didn't want to end this
But you already had

PERSPECTIVE

'Situationships'

I've seen a few times in meme's - "IM NOT READY FOR A RELATIONSHIP" (with you). How many times have you heard these words: 'I'm not ready for a relationship'? The 'with you' at the end is silent. A 'situationship' is unsafe. It has no direction and is full of confusion. Mixed emotions, no title, no real structured plan or commitment. Just another option until a better one comes along. If you're in one of these situations, you need to ask yourself if this is what you want. If it suits you, that's great! But if you want what you have to develop into something serious, that's where it gets complicated. That's when you need to think about stepping back.

The problem is, it can be quite difficult to tell if we're in a 'situationship' or a relationship. Both can feel quite similar. You spend time together, laugh, and are intimate with each other. But you can have all this without actually being TOGETHER. When we get into these situations, we feel like we are in control. We trick ourselves into thinking that we're unattached, immune to the hurt and pain that actual relationships often bring.

PART 7: PRESSURE AND MANIPULATION

But are we really immune? Are we really unattached?

How would you feel, for example, about the person you're in a 'situationship' with speaking to other women? Are you entitled to feel anything? There's no set plan here, no rules. You're not in a committed relationship. They want you, only when they want you. They can be charming when they want to be, but they can't support any of your goals and dreams, can't help you or motivate you to achieve them because they can't actually do any of those things even for themselves. Are we expecting stability and love from unstable and unlovable people? Are we in a 'situationship'? Are we just sailing with the wind and hoping to dock in at relationship central? Relationships are intentional and both of you need to be on the same page. Don't get me wrong, I'm not saying you have to be exactly what each other wants. Nope! We're not chasing fairytales, remember. What I'm saying is, if you have the same relationship goals, then you have a foundation on which to build and achieve those goals. Sometimes you'll both need to find ways to compromise when disagreements inevitably arise, but this isn't the same as accepting yellow or red flags (more on this below). If you can show mutual love and respect, then it's a win. If not, keep that ship on the water. You can jump off and swim to any island.

How often do we accept negative relationships and just settle? At what point do our emotions take over? At what point, do we start feeling confused, unworthy, questioning ourselves about what we want, what we deserve. Or was it just a big lack of communication from the get-go and a load of exciting feelings that took over and misled us? When we start feeling as though we are doing everything in a relationship without actually being in one, we have to reassess our expectations.

Except, we don't have any entitlement to even have anything to say because we're not in a relationship. It's just a one-sided situation. At what point after you start 'situationing' (seeing that person) do you think or question the following:
How do I feel about them?
Do I enjoy spending time with them?
Do they impact me in a positive or negative way?

PART 7: PRESSURE AND MANIPULATION

Are there any yellow flags?

Are there any red flags?

How do you feel when you leave them?

Make a tick list for every one of these feelings you encounter ✅

Nervous

Excited

Drained

Missed

Relieved

Dependant

Unsure

Suspicious

Happy

Encouraged

Motivated

Inspired

Angry

Sad

Depleted

Jealous

Loved

PERSPECTIVE

Joy

Disgust

This sort of simple exercise can help you to decide whether a 'situationship' is working for you. Are the negatives outweighing the positives? If so, it could be time to leave.

Chemistry

You can be single/in a relationship/ married/ divorced and still have chemistry with someone else. So, what is chemistry? Basically, chemistry is a feeling of connection, of bonding with someone on more than a superficial level. Chemistry is about attraction, usually (but not always) involving physical attraction as well as personality. Chemistry is when someone lights your candle with their flame.

Chemistry can be a great thing, leading from anything from short-term fun to meaningful relationships. However, allowing someone to 'light your fire' has the potential to become a highly flammable situation. When we have chemistry with someone, we can make rash decisions based on short-term happiness and excitement. 'Spur of the moment' actions can be great, and I'm not saying that every single decision you make has to be carefully thought out. Being spontaneous with someone new in your life can be fun, but you need to be aware that your actions can sometimes backfire, causing pain and hurt.

When you experience chemistry with someone, think about the context. Where did the encounter happen?
Whilst being intoxicated?
At work?
On the street?
In a shop?
With a friend or group of friends?
With your partner?

We meet people all the time, have encounters every-day – depending on your job or your hobbies. Some people don't meet people frequently and this is also a problem that causes them to become too reliant on that feeling of chemistry. Just because you get on with someone, it doesn't mean they're going to turn out to be your true love. Embrace chemistry, but don't let it cloud your judgement, and don't count on it as something that will sustain a 'situationship'.

Lies

When I started writing this section, I wanted to say, 'why do men lie?' But women lie too. It's human nature, something we do to protect ourselves, make ourselves look better, or just make life a bit easier. Sometimes the lie might be so close to the truth, we don't even acknowledge that we're lying! 'Bending the truth', 'little white lies' – we have lots of phrases to make lying seem more acceptable. I'd be a liar if I said I've never lied. I absolutely have lied. When I looked at it deeper and explored why I lied, and what I lied about, I came up with this list of reasons and excuses:

Sick day or / Late for work - an excuse

To not make myself look bad

To cover up that I don't always have my mornings together

To cover up that I was late for the school run as well

To cover up that I'm not coping as a parent sometimes

PART 7: PRESSURE AND MANIPULATION

To cover up any kind of flaw that can leave me vulnerable or depleted

I would like to say that my timing is impeccable. However, looking at how many times I may have used the above lines showed me I wasn't as good as I thought. Which is why I lied in the first place. Which means I already subconsciously knew. When we are proud and happy with our truths we shout and share them. When it's our not so good side, we keep it to ourselves or share it with only a select few. We lie about all sorts of things for all sorts of reasons: to get ahead, to secure a job (for example, by lying on our CV), to impress others, to keep a relationship going. The list goes on.

Because I'm not a person who intentionally wants to do any harm or damage, I find it hard to think of lying in a manipulative or sneaky way, as something we do to get a desired outcome. Like many people, I'm very nice. I want to help, advise, make a situation better or find a solution to a problem. To make new friends and to connect on greater levels. To uplift and figure out life with in-depth conversations.

PERSPECTIVE

On the flip side of that (the ying and yang – two sides to everything), I can be really direct and unapologetically sharp. This has to be triggered in me. It happens when I'm provoked in some way, even if the person on the receiving end of my sharp tongue didn't mean to provoke me. This is a defence mode I use to protect myself.

Learning and growing within myself has shown me that not everything needs a reaction, even when triggered. By always reacting to my triggers, I was handing control over to whoever provoked me. If this sounds familiar, I advise you to work on becoming aware of your triggers. Only by being honest to yourself about your triggers will you find a way to control them. Otherwise, other people will have control over you.

PART 8: RE-EDUCATING OURSELVES

What we learn as kids doesn't necessarily match up with what we need to know as adults in order to have happy, fulfilling lives. In this chapter, I want to talk about what's lacking in our childhood education and upbringings, and how this can negatively impact us in later life. Throughout this chapter, a common theme will be that learning never stops – we learn from all kinds of situations in life, the good and the bad. Everything is a learning opportunity, and we should embrace those opportunities when they come our way.

The playground situation: roundabouts, slides, and see-saws

The roundabout is a metaphor I like to use to describe going round and round dealing with the same bullshit. Nothing changes or gets resolved. The types of bullshit you have to deal with on the roundabout may come in different shapes and forms, but in essence, it's still the same old shit. Jumping off can feel scary and overwhelming, but it's something you have to do in order to begin learning from those negatives. The slide represents set-backs – progress followed by failure in equal measure. You make a big climb, putting those problems further and further behind you, until the next choice has you sliding down right back to where you started. The see-saw represents those ups and downs we all experience. It's a bumpy ride; one minute you're feeling great, flying in the air, next minute you bump to the ground, the shock-waves vibrating through your whole body! The comedown is much greater than the upwards swing, leaving you with a sore bum from the dramatic drop. In other words, the joy is temporary, but the negative effects stick around for a while. Nothing really great comes from playing at the park these days – the fun and freedom is outside the bars. These play-grounds were made for supervision by someone wiser who guides you and tells you what you need to do, who cheers you on when you make it down the slide. Every achievement should be met with love and encourage-ment. When we become older and decide to play in the park, we have to realise that we are there with no su-pervision. We have to ask ourselves: do we really want what we think we want? Every day you need to make a conscious effort to work on your mental strength. To maintain calm, even when feeling anxious. To remain in control of thoughts so they don't fly around erratically. Maintaining daily standards about things that matter to us.

School lessons vs life lessons

I have always questioned what 'life school' really teaches us about ourselves. Our emotions. Our brains. What we think and how we think. School teaches us maths, English, and a load of other stuff that's either missing information, as with history, or misconstrued information, like the idea that Jesus is white, which is taught to most of us in Religious Education (no offence intended to any other opinions of Jesus' race). But really, what does school teach us other than a lot of things we will likely never use in daily life? I'm not completely disregarding school, but in my opinion, teaching everyone the same thing in the same way as if there are no different learning and thinking strategies is not a good thing. Dull, repetitive teaching strategies take away creativity and individuality, when we should in fact be encouraging these things in our children.

PERSPECTIVE

What school teaches:

Algebra

Shakespeare

Photosynthesis

Restricted history

A how-to guide in bullying or being a victim

What school should teach:

What emotions are and what role they play in various scenarios

Critical and reflective thinking

Understanding ourselves and others

How to socialise

Mental health

To embrace uniqueness

Relationships of all kinds: family, friends, love, etc.

How to handle money, personal finances, assets and liabilities

How to start a business

Personality traits and awareness of self

Fitness and healthy living

How to defend yourself

PART 8: RE-EDUCATING OURSELVES

Out of this list, how many can you say that you've been taught? And who taught you? Parents, teachers, friends? Where did they learn the things they taught you? Most of the things you've learnt (especially at school) have been taught to you from someone else's perspective. Who's to say that their perspective is correct? If the things you've learned from others has helped you in any way, that's great! But if you're reading this, something's missing, right? I felt so too. Deeply. I didn't feel as though I was learning much that was relevant to my happiness and well-being while I was at school. So, without much guidance, I went in search of happiness and success by myself. My idea of happiness was 'in a relationship' – it's as if the only times I regarded as being happy were the really great loving moments that I replay in my mind repeatedly. Those moments when you're creating core memories and just don't want the moment or the feeling to go anywhere. You want it to last forever.

To put it simply, my happiness depended on another person. Their love and attention were everything to me, and when I didn't receive it, it felt like my happiness was non-existent. This is why it's so important to have happiness that comes just from you, that can't be taken away when someone you love leaves or lets you down.

Growing up, I wasn't encouraged to like myself. The values we are taught at school reinforce the idea that our achievements make us likeable. Doing well in lessons and in sports were praiseworthy things, but if you didn't like those things, or weren't good at them, you were treated as a 'bad person' – by other kids and teachers.

I can't recall ever being told to think positively about myself. No wonder it's such a struggle to find self-love if we're told from the beginning that we're worth nothing more than our so-called achievements. We are told to treat each other fairly, that everyone is different. We are told to embrace our uniqueness, and to be our-selves. And yet, when we deviate from the social norms taught to us at school, we're excluded, we're disliked, we're told to change. For many people, this continues into adult life. You have to dig deep to accept your uniqueness. You have to put your feelings about who you are first instead of listening to what other people tell you to be. This is a hard lesson, one that lots of people never learn. We are told to be happy and told not to be sad. But no one tells us what happiness is, or why it isn't ok to feel sad.

I always ask my clients, 'what makes you happy?'. There are rules to this question: It can't be another person, it can't be items you have or want to buy, it can't be money. Give me 3 answers. When you apply these rules, most people find it difficult to come up with answers. In short, they don't know what makes them happy beyond these things. But if I ask you to give me five different things that makes someone else happy, like your mum, dad, partner, kids, or siblings, you've got a list of ten, maybe even fifteen, answers. It seems that answering the question for ourselves is much more difficult than answering for others. This relates to the self-love theme; we find it much easier to love others (and therefore understand the things that make others happy) than to love ourselves.

PERSPECTIVE

Before reading this next section, I suggest grabbing a pen and paper. Write down three things that make you happy (paying attention to the above rules).

I'll wait for you, or write it here in the space below:

I'll tell you mine. First, the sun: It's free, it's beautiful, and it's always there. It provides warmth. Second, my eyes: I'm so grateful for them. It seems a small thing to be grateful for, but my eyesight isn't fantastic. I look forward to improving it, but without glasses or contact lenses, I wouldn't be able to see properly. I value my eyes and my capacity to see things, from a facial expression to a morning gesture, and from a sunset to all of life's experiences. This indeed makes me happy.

Sometimes it's hard to think back on my whole nearly thirty years of life. So much of it has been coloured by misunderstanding. Sometimes it feels like I've wasted so much time, or didn't do what everyone else had done or was doing. I felt so angry and negative about everything. But that's an old perspective. The new perspective is that I have learnt so much and experienced so many different things, from the smallest lesson to the biggest one. My perspective moved from hurt and blame to taking responsibility and learning for myself, so I wouldn't get frustrated with others for not knowing me. They should know me! They should know how I am! This is what I used to think. But how could they know me, if I didn't know myself? How could they help me, if I didn't reach out and share my problems?

Learning through relationships

It was towards the end of 2015 that I decided I was going to change my life. I wasn't sure really what I was going to do. But I decided that I was going to make some major changes.

Adulting timeline

I've already discussed my childhood and time at school, so let's start from 2005.

2005 - nearly permanently excluded from school / worked in a sun bed shop in Croydon

2006 - allowed to do GCSE's / finish school / worked as a clerk in estate agents / met my first boyfriend (not the V taker) but my daughter's dad.

2007 - went to college (with him)

PART 8: RE-EDUCATING OURSELVES

2008 - worked for Mothercare and ELC, then went on to work for Halfords – then I became pregnant/prepared to move out and become somewhat independent (though looking back I realise I was dependent on my partner and the bubble we'd created for ourselves).

2009 - became a mum / moved around a bit from temporary places: a studio flat in South Norwood to a two bed flat above a shop in Sydenham, then to a beautiful house in lower Sydenham (where, incidentally, I fell down the stairs, which caused me to go into labour). I am 19 and doing my best to furnish my home and keep it looking and feelng nice, but I'm struggling to do everything by myself financially. Everything household-related falls to me, with no help from my partner. You'd think that when someone 'loves you' they'd help you in all ways possible. But this isn't what I experienced from my partner. It was give, give, give from me. At the same time, I felt I literally had to do anything and everything for him in order to show my love (within reason). It was a double standard that I'd created for myself, and it was wearing me down. At the time, I would have said I was the perfect 'desperate housewife'. I cooked, I cleaned, I did the shopping, I ensured

PERSPECTIVE

that bills were in order and prioritised. DAMMIT I WAS THE MAN AND THE WOMAN! Looking back, I ask myself these questions: What was his version of love? What was his version of a relationship? What was his version of what a woman should be doing for a man, and what a man should do for a woman? Now, I intend no disrespect when talking about this relationship. I'm not saying that all men are like him and all women are like I was. I'm just telling my story, from my perspective. This is the whole purpose of my book, to give a perspective on things that many of us are faced with daily. Things that we struggle with, mentally and emotionally. My mission here is to address the question, 'what if?'. What if we all knew this stuff, before we had to go through it ourselves? What if we could learn from someone else's story?

Pain

I want some recognition
For the pain I sometimes feel
I know it's my responsibility
To make the move to heal

The pain goes through my body
Like the lightning through the rain
I didn't think this cloud
Would come back round again

It's such a shame I feel this pain
Self-inflicted as I loved again
A single vision
With no provision

In all it teaches
Is strength and pain
To tear us down for 'love' again

From open reaches
A drowning soul
And put on high alert control

PERSPECTIVE

To numb it out
We scream
We shout
The silence drowns the noises out

When no one hears
Or sees the tears
You're all alone and faced with fears

You made it out
Without a doubt
And that's what healing's
All about

So, we make it clear
Let it disappear
It has no home or loving here

We all feel pain
Maybe in vain
But that's the choice we make again

We have control
So, take it back
have this note and read it back

PART 8: RE-EDUCATING OURSELVES

Back to basics

The problems I experienced in my home and in my relationship I think came down, in part, to the way men and women learn what it means to 'be a woman' or what it means to 'be a man'. Even looking back in history, men are the bread-winners (money) and women the bread makers (housewife). In traditional relationships, women usually organise and regulate the house, which involves so many different tasks and responsibilities. These typically include:

Shopping

Cooking and preparing meals

Cleaning

Looking after the children, which has a whole list of tasks on its own

But men have so much to think about too: how to be the breadwinner, and how to be a man. Generally speaking, moving out of the home for men isn't as easy as it is for women. If they're not taught how to do basic household tasks from a young age, how will they manage alone? We must raise our children – regardless of gender – to be able to live in this world without

PERSPECTIVE

us. I need to know that if I was gone tomorrow, I would have instilled a certain amount of self-resilience in my daughter. Female empowerment. Manners. Hygiene. Standards. House standards. Chore standards. Running a household.

They say teach them young, and we are so quick to give them an extra curriculum lesson outside of school. Yet somehow, we manage to miss all of the above. 'It's ok! My kid is an excellent piano player and top in karate', you might argue. But this doesn't mean much if your child has no manners or respect. The same goes with adults. We can earn all the money, get jobs, have nice houses, have lots of Instagram friends, have the desired lifestyle. However, when we are not aware of some basic things, like happiness, respect, and how to look after ourselves (practically and emotionally), how much does all that other stuff really matter? When we spend more of our time working on the mask we wear for the rest of the world to see than on what's going on inside and in private, that's when we have a problem.

At what age should we start instilling these basic values in our children? Some would say they pick things up as they go along, that basic tasks like cooking can be learned in adulthood, once they've left home. However, when a child has the capacity to learn something, it doesn't make sense to delay teaching them. For example, they can learn to walk from as early as 7-12 months, but we wouldn't delay teaching them to walk because they can learn that later in life, would we? And yet, we have a generation of adults (mainly men, I would say) who don't know how to keep a home.

I'm not sticking up for men who are too lazy to do much around the house. But in my opinion and experience, I believe they are less equipped than women to do these sorts of tasks because they weren't ever taught. The blame lies partly with them, but also with their upbringing. Women also have it hard, in the sense that we're expected to juggle everything. It used to be the case women took care of stuff in the home, but now we're expected to do that while also having a job. We are expected to do everything the man does and also look after the kids, the home, potential pets (don't underestimate that responsibility), and daily life. Women who do all this are queens and everyday heroes. Those men who take on the 'women's responsibilities' are also crowned kings.

Doing a traditionally female task, or taking on a traditionally female role, doesn't make you less of a man, but more of one. It comes down to self-confidence, of having it in you to be a supportive presence in your partner's life. As we discussed earlier, this doesn't mean throwing money at them, it means helping with the washing-up, putting your kid to bed, all those little things that add up to something much bigger. It's easy to separate men and women into different categories based on their roles, behaviours, and preferences, but this is too simple. Both need to be kind, supportive, and loving, and these are the things we should focus on in any relationship – not on who should do the washing-up! There are things happening in everyone's life on a daily basis that we don't even think twice about because we simply have no standards on how we should be treated and spoken to. We lack knowledge about self-love and self-care. To me, loving yourself was a bad thing growing up. No one seemed to like people who thought they were a good person. To other people, liking yourself meant you must have thought that you were better than everyone. But self-love isn't about comparing yourself to others and behaving as if you're better than they are. It's about accepting yourself, understanding yourself, and not falling into the trap, that so many of us fall into, of beating yourself up on a daily basis.

Recognising red flags

Pay attention to the red flags – I call these red flags the 'relationshits'. We see red flags, but so often we ignore them. We blind ourselves, painting the red flags yellow so that we don't have to deal with them. However, it's important that we recognise red flags for what they are and that we react to them. So, what do I mean by 'red flags'? Red flags can refer to lots of different behaviours. However, in this section, I'm going to talk about them in relation to sex. Why is sex so powerful? What have we been taught about sex, other than the basics? What were you taught?

PERSPECTIVE

Lessons from sex

Looking back, I can't really remember being taught. I remember some aspects of sex education in primary school, but it never felt like a serious subject. Especially onboard a giraffe bus, with lots of childlike stuff inside discussing something that's actually quite serious. We treated sex education as a funny topic to disguise the cringe and embarrassment that went with it.

Even now, sex is sometimes deemed a dirty subject to talk about. This is especially true when it comes to parents teaching their kids about it. They don't like the idea of their kid thinking about sex, so they don't teach them much about it. Obviously, this is the wrong approach, and leads to lots of misunderstanding and misconduct when kids get older. So, why is sex such a taboo subject when it comes to learning about it? Why is it not spoken about? I think we NEED to talk about it. The less we talk openly about sex, the more things happen behind the scenes because people feel like it's only them experiencing some things. I think the bad outweighs the good when it comes to talking, even if it can sometimes feel a bit embarrassing. Let's break it down. What comes from sex:

Good things: boosts libido, a desirable feeling/sensation, energy, passion, burning calories, love, connection, increased confidence, pregnancy and childbirth, an increase in self-worth.

Bad things: illusion of love, unplanned pregnancy, domestic violence, rape, STDs and STIs, a decrease in self-worth. A sexual connection is more than just "doing the deed". This is where soul ties come in and emotional connections – even connections and behaviours that we don't even realise. It's scary. I know that once I have sex with someone – especially if it's someone I like a lot, the connection is serious.

I've had a couple one-night stands, as they call them, and to be honest I would have at some point regretted them. But each one showed me something about myself and about the men I was with. They helped me make better decisions later down the road. Those one-night stands aren't something I'm proud of, even if I don't regret them. They didn't match with what I wanted, which was to have a baby and get married and build a life with one person. Sometimes what we want and what happens isn't always what is planned. I make much better decisions as I get older, but I feel I owe this at least in part to those earlier mistakes. When writing about something so personal, I say 'bare all', but I'm struggling. I'm struggling with myself, with laying myself bare for anyone to read. It makes me feel vulnerable. But also sets me free.

Rape, drugs, and alcohol

I want to talk about rape, drugs, and alcohol, and how these things relate to sex and the decisions we make about sex. "How many drinks will it take you to leave with me?" (Shouts to Miguel for the tune). Yes ladies, we sing along, but have we actually listened to the lyrics? You might argue that song lyrics aren't important, that they really don't mean anything and shouldn't be taken seriously. Music in a club or bar is just music, intended to create a vibe. But lyrics come from somewhere, and they send out a message. So, let's consider the question posed by Miguel: How many drinks will it take you to leave with him (the guy at the bar)? Until you have enough to forget yourself and be taken advantage of, is usually the answer.

This ties in with the subject of escapism. Drugs and alcohol can make us feel as though we are leaving our troubles behind, but really all they do is get us into deeper trouble. Temporarily forgetting about your problems, or becoming numb to them, can weaken your resolve to actually deal with those problems. If you rely on them to form relationships with others, this should be a red flag.

DOWNLOADABLE PRINTABLE AT

WWW.PERSPECTIVEBOOKSHOP.COM

PART 9: RE-DISCOVERING HAPPINESS

Breaking negative cycles

When I broke through my first negative cycle in 2016, I was at my breaking point. After I moved house and returned from a birthday trip to Amsterdam, I realised that I really had to take control of myself and my eating – especially since my daughter was diagnosed with Type 1 diabetes. As you might remember from an earlier chapter, this happened to be the same weekend that I found out my partner at the time had also been in hospital with his new baby. What a week, to say the least.

The emotions you are feeling have to be explored. Until then, you won't know what they're about. This gives us a deeper sense of ourselves, and of what drives our negative emotions – rage, anger, hurt, and so on. Until we deal with our emotional baggage, we will always carry it around with us, or sweep it 'under the rug', so to speak.

PERSPECTIVE

I only started to look into myself at age 26, age 29 at writing this book and over 30 when releasing. I'm still learning and growing by the day, with occasional pauses and setbacks, which we have to allow. It's great to distract ourselves by doing stuff with friends or family, or looking for your ex-partner in another man. But distracting ourselves from negative emotions places us in a cycle, preventing us from dealing with them. Usually, the original wound is the most painful. But it's the healing that hurts more than the wound. This is why so many of us prefer to stay in the cycle. It might be miserable and unfulfilling, but the pain is dull, easier to cope with than the raw, sharp pain that comes with confronting the negatives in our past.

What do you see for your future? For me, it helped not to look too far ahead. Before you start your day, make sure it has already been planned – same thing with the week, month, and year. This plan is just a provision, to be added to as you go along, and altered to make room for unexpected changes. Keep sight of what you want. Or, if you don't know what you want, take some time to figure it out. Make that your goal. Try new things, do stuff alone. This is key to figuring out what you want and developing confidence – which is a skill by the way.

Before I launched my business, I had scheduled some trips to prepare me for my vision. The first one I was anxious and had a panic attack or two. The times after were so easy, because I knew I was ok, knew I could do it. It was my own brain detecting danger (fear) and giving me more thoughts on top the other negative thoughts I already had. Practise as regularly as possible to be aware of what you do and what you tell yourself. This will help you to take control of your emotions and reactions.

The goal is to be more understanding of you. Loving yourself and understanding yourself doesn't come overnight. But gradual, consistent understanding will lead you to your most powerful you. You are going to make one of two choices: to go forward or simply make a choice to go back. Now apply that to everything! I'm just another human making choices and learning. I am responsible. I am helpful. I am loving. I am caring. I

PERSPECTIVE

can share what I know and what I am continually learning not only about me, but about life. Good luck with
your goals and plans and choices. Time flies. Make the
most of it.

Reflecting lying in the field

I think about it some days
I think about it now
When lying in the field
That is yet to be ploughed

It's imperfections slightly hidden
As clear as a big vision
Only fears are hidden
As I lay here in the field

Look up at the stars
And grab them one by one
The dream can't be a reality
If all you do is run

So, lay right here beside me
I'm hidden so come find me
It's amazing what can happen
When lying in the field

My vision I can see it
Its only mine to see
No one else can direct me
Even if for free

PERSPECTIVE

When guided by the spirits
The faith the love the glow
There's nothing to stop me lying here
Not even the snow

PART 9: RE-DISCOVERING HAPPINESS

Overcoming pain and finding happiness

I don't know when my pain stopped. It eventually dissolves when you replay the memories so many times you see them for what they actually are. This is exactly what happened to me after looking back on my relationship and going over the ups and downs in my head. We may have laughed or been happy in that moment, but how many moments are there like that in the day? You can replay a 15 second moment from a whole 24 hr day and 7-day week, forgetting that that was the good part. Man! It's as if the pain just drifts on, each memory replayed for the rest of time. When I think of the pure love I had for someone, I have to question, was it pure love? Was it unconditional, or was it a desperate love? I think I know the answer, but I can't be 100% sure even to this day. Who are we once we fall in love? Are we different? What happens when we let our guard down? Who do we become? Can we be ourselves – our real self? No hiding? When we fall in love again, is it for real, or do we just want to recreate those good times, those good moments? To feel good. To connect. To vibe. To be happy.

PERSPECTIVE

What is happiness and where do I find it? It's something I've looked into for a number of years. Here's a list of some of the different things I looked into:

Law of attraction

Affirmations

Vision boards

Motivational videos

Gym

Yoga

Meditation

As I discussed in Part 4, "Great Days Only" became my everyday go-to regardless of what happened on that day. That motivational saying came from within me, which makes all the difference. External motivation is great, but you can't rely on that alone. Use other people's motivation, just be sure to find your own too.

Freed

I used to think that I have so much to say that I have no words. I'm not being heard anyway, so what's the point in using my voice? Silence is better if I don't have anything positive to say. I've since learned that this was the wrong attitude. Communicating my problems to others and myself is important in resolving them. Otherwise, they fester away inside, making it more and more difficult to deal with them when they eventually become too much.

These days, I try to address things within 24-48 hours of when they happen. The temptation to ignore a problem is always there, so setting a time limit to deal with things helps me to get on and do it. As I discussed earlier, how you handle things and what you choose to accept sets a standard for how people treat you. I finally disclosed what was actually going on back in 2016, after that horrible year. I told a friend. I disclosed what I thought was my shame. My embarrassment. My pride. My ego. Everything was bruised. I had to show these internal markings of hurt and disappointment somehow and, for me, the way to do this was by talking about it. I was crushed. It had felt so long since I had felt like this, and everything I was scared of came right round to get me. Here I am again, I thought to myself. As the hurt and anger resided, I felt my tears fall. The only good thing about this not being the first time my heart's been broken is that I know it doesn't last forever. Nothing ever does.

Time the healer

This is the last thing anyone ever wants to hear. Healing takes time and space; it doesn't happen overnight. It gets easier with time because there are only so many times you can think about something and feel sad about it. The effects of that hurt become weaker over time, less able to influence your mood. Whether you've experienced your first heartbreak or your twentieth, love hurts the same, and we need to give ourselves time to heal. Things become easier over time because we change within ourselves. I think this is due to becoming used to new surroundings, and to new ways of being. It's common to fear the possibility that love will never come to us again. A love that you held for that person who is no longer your person might feel irreplaceable. But what if there's better? We have to allow ourselves to believe that there's more for us. Our stories don't have to end with heartbreak.

Acknowledging that time is a great healer doesn't mean you have to put up with being unhappy in the short-term, however. If you are not happy with something that is happening in your life, you don't have to wait until some unspecified date in the future to vent about it. You could take a closer look and realise that, what is now annoying you won't even matter in a day or two, and that spending any time at all cursing your circumstances is a big waste of your time. Instead of stewing internally about whatever's hurting or annoying you, try writing your thoughts down. Some might say 'Really Tara?! Write about it? I wanna rip someone's head off!'. Just try it. The next thing that annoys you. Journal it. And keep it to yourself. Then write something positive. Like, what you enjoy doing, or what's coming up that you're looking forward to, or what do you want to make happen? Let's get the ball point rolling (I hope you see what I did there!).

PERSPECTIVE

<u>Keep your heart</u>

I hurt
I throbbed
I ached
I sobbed
It had felt like a whole heart was just robbed.

I can't say mine as it had no name
I just saw the damage,
Surely someone's to blame.

It has to be mine.
I seek to find.

A vain attempt to give it life.
I grabbed it hard and held it tight.
I was about
to put everything right.

My heart you're mine
It will be fine
Just get across the finish line,
You still have beat, some love and rhythm.
I feel it in me. I must be winning.

I thought I died,

I must be dead.

To trust and learn to love again.

It must be done, you should not run.

Your life has only just begun.

So, take this heart

And place it back

Your soul will put it right intact.

So, thank us now the lessons ended.

Be sure not to go back pretending.

We have one life and many lessons.

Don't take your heart out,

it's such a blessing.

PERSPECTIVE

Distancing ourselves from drama

One topic I want to discuss in this section is drama. People who say they don't want drama are usually the ones who create it. Drama is not something I'm prepared to tolerate these days, so if someone starts creating it, I distance myself from it. Drama is a waste of energy and drains everyone involved. People will try to drag you into it, whether at home or work, but you have to make a choice about how far you want to get involved. Some people might think that drama is a way of exposing negative issues, of communicating problems. But in my experience, drama stokes up problems, inflaming them until they're out of control. Much better to talk sensibly and openly about a problem, without all the dramatic flair that often goes with it.

I'm not always positive, but I try to be the best I can. Some days I have to remind myself I've made all these positive changes for myself and can lose it all in a second for someone who isn't worth it. Things I'm seeing differently now: Not worrying or overthinking, complete peace of mind, not worrying about other women.

PART 9: RE-DISCOVERING HAPPINESS

It's taken me a long time to realise it, but drama and happiness don't go hand in hand. When people create drama, it's actually just another form of manipulation, of trying to get a reaction from you. The more you resist the urge to rise to it, the easier it will be to reach a point where you don't ever feel the need to rise to it.

PART 10: HEALED PEOPLE HEAL

In this last part, I'm going to give you a snapshot into my life on a day where I was feeling great about everything. This was the day that inspired me to start writing this book. It's the 17th of December 2018 and I feel amazing. I've got a day off work, and I have the space I need to really think about a lot of things – things about myself that I know I need to change or that I want to look deeper into.

Sometimes, I really have to check myself, because when I feel happy, I almost become overwhelmed with all the amazing things in my life. I'm so grateful for my life and for the courage it's given me, the courage to be myself and to reach out to other people.

Placing yourself

I want to help others so much, but I need those people to want to help themselves first. A lot of people don't want to help themselves, which is when I start getting frustrated. I want to take people on my journey, but I find that hard to deal with if they're not willing to accept my help. I even start having moments of self-doubt. I have to remind myself not to fall into negative patterns when trying to help others. I'll do what I can for other people, but I have to put myself first and lead by example.

Putting myself first isn't me being selfish or mean. It doesn't mean that I don't love anybody, because I do, deeply. But to be of any use in helping others, I have to focus on myself, and I'm really understanding that now. I feel really strong and confident in myself. I'm trying to be happy because it's difficult – at least, sometimes it can be. Happiness should be easy, but it's something I have to make an effort to focus on because of the way my mind is conditioned. Happiness is a state of mind you choose to be in; it can't be bought – not in the long-term, anyway. Knowledge is power, but only when that knowledge is applied. It isn't enough to know our faults and negativities, we have to actively work on them, which is something I'm trying to do. There is so much in me that wants to do so much for other people. That's absolutely amazing and fantastic, and I love that about myself. But then I kind of start forgetting about myself and all the things I'm trying to do for me. When this happens, it means I'm not doing all the things I'm telling other people to do, which doesn't make sense. So, I'm deciding that I just need to start putting myself first, putting my daughter first, putting my home first, put in all MY things first.

I've started sewing recently, and my daughter started with me. She loves it and wants to start making clothes for other kids. I might even think about making a little business out of our new hobby. I love being creative, doing something just for me, without worrying about what other people think. The fact that I can share this with my daughter is even better. I can't tell you to follow my example in doing the things that make me happy and fulfilled. And I need to stop worrying if what works for me doesn't work for someone else. Unless someone reaches out and asks for my help, there's not much I can do or say. In buying/borrowing this book, you've reached out, and I hope you've found something useful in these pages.

The world is in our hands

It was dark
It was late
I stayed up
And then I ate

I ate it out of comfort.
Eating it with ease
A second on my lips
A million by my knees

I wondered when you'd get home
And if you'd tell me lies
Lies of where you've been all night
This was no surprise

In and through the day
And how many girls you'd see
Whilst you were laying down with me
I'm one
She's two
She's three

PERSPECTIVE

When it's time to come home
I'm always fast asleep
A quick brush teeth and shower
And in our dream we'd meet

I'd tell you that I love you
That things will work out fine
The pain from intuition
I knew that I had lied

Lied to say it's ok
That it will work out fine
When all along I really knew
he wasn't even mine

For he was lost himself
Writing in the sand
It's only when the tide comes in
It clears all of the land

The writing disappears
Like all the hurt and pain
Unless you decided to hold it
And go back round again

The choice is yours as always
It's given free to all
It's only when the love bomb comes
He doesn't seem so cruel

The thought of getting dragged in
Back and forth we go
We didn't see the red flags
We went round and passed go

Choices come in all things
Even when we sleep
What we choose
And who we love
It can only go so deep

So, when we wake up daily
It's always in our hands
What we do and what we choose
The world is in our hands

PERSPECTIVE

It's hard for me to stay silent when I come across people who could clearly use a bit of help. I have to keep reminding myself that things that seem obvious to me aren't always obvious to others. I have to try not to get annoyed when other people seem to lack common sense. All I can do is try and understand, but that's a two-way process because they have to want to be understood. I can offer guidance, but only when I'm asked. Sometimes it feels very much like I'm trying to be everybody's life coach and at times have to step back and just be the friend or family member. Life coaching/mentoring has recently become one of my business ventures, which is a good way of keeping coaching separate from my personal life. I do this alongside mentoring and vision boards. And on top of all that, I'm always there for family and friends who have things they need to talk about. I've come to realise that investing in myself is an important step in investing in others. I can't help anyone if *I'm* a mess! Finding new hobbies, working on your career, going to the gym – all those sorts of things – are ways of investing in your-self. I've been saying it throughout this book, and I'll say it again now: Great Days Only! It doesn't matter what's around the corner, it's about what you say and do in the present. Today. My journey towards healing has helped me to heal others. I'm not always perfect – sometimes my advice can come across as abrupt or even uncaring. That's something I need to work on. I also need to work on anger management, because that's definitely something that is still a part of my life, even if it's a smaller part than it used to be. In life, there are many kinds of suffering. But we have to use our suffering to make things better for ourselves. Bad experiences are learning opportunities, and we should use each and every one of them. Even now, I sometimes fall back into reclusive behaviour when I feel a certain way. While it's important not to hide away, I've also realised that I don't need to pressure myself into always going out. I prefer quiet spaces to big crowds, and heavy drinking and partying has never really been me. On this particular day, in this snapshot in time, I feel great about myself. I look nice. My hair's nice. I look healthy. I've got a little bit of makeup on. I've got that glow – I feel good. Everything's working out for me now. I'm in a much better place than I was this time last year. Back then, I was going through the whole heartache of my previous relationship. At the time, I couldn't believe it had really come to an end. But now, I realise it was a good end, a positive turning point in my life. I'd been trying to leave him for months, and he never once made it easy. He'd turn up at my house, that sort of thing. But I came out on top in the end. I've done stuff that I want to do, and there's more I plan on doing. I love doing stuff with my daughter, and I still want to get her into other things and give her the opportunity to try anything she wants (within reason!). She's got a list. So, I've started helping her work on that list, getting things up and running, being support- ive of her hobbies. I've also been trying hard to support her health and diet, paying attention to the things she needs in order to manage her diabetes in the best ways possible. I really need to think about the whole food sit- uation (transitioning to a vegan diet) because although I'm happy being vegan, it can also be quite stressful. Not only do I have to make decisions for me and my daughter regarding what's best for us and our health, but we also have have self-control when socialising around everybody else who eats meat and all the other things that we're trying to make a big change from.

The pig story

It can be difficult to introduce changes into your life when you're still around people who do all the things you're trying to move away from. It's like a story I once read, where the little pig that lives at home, does everything his family does – rolling around in the mud and eating rubbish. When the pig grows up into a big pig, he leaves home and he ends up going to all the amazing pig shows and doing all of the positive things everyone else is doing in these new environments. Basically, the pig emulates his surroundings, picking up all the bad habits of the people around him in old environments. But as a big pig out in the big wide world, he's able to learn more things too, using his new experiences to shape him into a different pig from the one that left home. Our home environment teaches us what's normal, and this means that what we learn at home, we take with us into adult life. When we leave home, we meet new people, experience new things, and generally grow as people. So, what happens to the pig when he returns home? Well, he shows off all the new things he's learned, and talks excitedly about what he's achieved. His friends and family are impressed, but they haven't grown and changed with the pig. So, what happens when the pig spends time with them? He gets all covered in mud again! This is what I felt like was happening to me. Whenever I met up with the people I'd been around before I made a positive change in my life, it felt like I was getting dragged back into the same old negative things – talking shit, eating rubbish. I'd try and talk about the new things I'd learned and experienced, but I wasn't really being listened to – it wasn't a topic of conversation for this crowd. Eating with them became a problem because, as I said, I was trying to get me and my daughter used to healthier foods, and this is so difficult when everyone else around you is eating junk.

This is why I made the decision to get out more and talk to people who are more similar to me or who are completely different to me. This is what my workshops and networking events are about; meeting like-minded people. It's great to be able to have genuine conversations about things I'm interested in without being on the defence. You can't change yourself if you're surrounded by the same people who dragged you into a negative way of thinking in the first place. You don't have to abandon those people, but you should think about removing yourself from them to an extent. If you want things to be different, you have to be different and live differently and stay focused on your things. And that is a very lonely place because it's just you and your goals and your targets. But that's the life. That's the choice. It's not forever... Just till you bloom. We find our passions individually, in different places and at different times. It's only right that you keep searching for what it is you want.

Don't settle. Don't stay sad, or mad, or wherever it is you happen to be. You are not a tree. You are not stuck. Yes, we all have commitments, but these commitments can be re-worked to fit with what works for you. You will almost certainly find obstacles in the pursuit of what you want, but what in life isn't an obstacle? We encounter them all the time, but we can't let them stop us. Go and find your joy. Life's too short to settle for anything less. And if you don't find joy where you expect to find it, look elsewhere, ask around, look within. Find it and hold onto it and let go of whatever doesn't bring you joy.

PERSPECTIVE

Trees

I am not perfect
And I will never be
It's like when we stand outside
And look out at the trees

They have sturdy bodies
Such grace and elegance

But it's when you get up close
You'll find unique presence

I am only a human
Comparing to a tree
But you see
I am not perfect and neither is he

I say he meaning humans
As we are all as one

An energy embrace alone
Can sometimes be no fun
So, time we share
And do not care
There's some out there that do compare

Be like me

Think of the tree

It's imperfect

Like you

And me

PERSPECTIVE

Words of affirmation I say to myself in my mind or out loud, or I write in my journals.

I like myself

I love myself

I am beautiful

I am confident

I am powerful

I am strong

I am kind

I am loving

I am helpful

I am my own fan

I inspire myself

I can do it

I can do it all

I am successful

I appreciate myself

I love me

I love all of me

I am the best

I love my work

I love how I create it all

I love how I know what I am wanting

I would look at myself in the mirror and repeat.

Write and keep journals. Create voice notes. I've found, no matter how many people I speak to, only I can help myself, other people may be able to aid that process but initially it comes from me. Then, the consistency keeps it going.

There are many printables that can be found online for free at www.perspectivebookshop.com

Our thoughts and reactions are like a stock room of stocked up memories and experiences. We have a BOARD OF MANAGERS of ourselves.

A happy part of you.

An angry part of you

The sad part of you

A disgusted part of you

The scared part of you

Every day, from when we open our eyes. The panel is always active.

This brain panel comes with us everywhere.

Though all experiences and all situations.

This panel technically decides how we will react or respond to people /situations/experiences. But the

PERSPECTIVE

panel of thought that introduces feeling (you have a thought first, then a feeling.) When any situations arise.

Thank you so much for reading my book. I hope it leaves you with a different perspective for yourself. You are amazing, strong and powerful. Strong enough to do and be anything you want. Take it from someone who never knew what it's like, let alone to make it out of the stigma of council flat estate kids. Which is a mindset!! Look at me. I'm an Author. All the best.

Tara Knowles

Printed in Great Britain
by Amazon